TELL HIM WITH YOUR HEART

RAYMOND H. FIKE, JR.

Tell Him With Your Heart

The Theme and Purpose of this Book is to Glorify God

*This is only a small glimpse into the true account and journey of Ray &
Sandi Fike and their two children. It was written by Ray Fike and inspired
by the word of God.*

Tell Him With Your Heart

I am so glad that God took the time
To form me and schedule my days

The many blessings and miracles described in this book
provide only a glimpse of all our Lord has done for us.

Through all the healings in our lives, there are also many times of need and suffering. This is not Heaven, for as the Apostle John declared, "It is not yet revealed what we will be; but we know that when he is revealed, we will be like him; for we will see him just as he is" (1 John 3:2). That is, when He comes and takes us away to paradise, we shall be like him. In Ecclesiastes 3, the Lord reveals that there is a time, place, and a season for all things, that He may be glorified. We are only one breath away from home.

Contents

FOREWORD

OURS IS A troubled world. We don't have to look far for a reason to be anxious or afraid. The growing threat of international terrorism leads us to question our safety as we dine out, visit a concert hall, or attend a sporting event. Then there are the more immediate, day-to-day concerns with keeping a job in a fragile economy, guarding our children's hearts in an X-rated society, caring for aging parents, and so on . . . and on. Into this world of trouble, we hear our Lord's voice, calm and gentle:

> "Let not your heart be troubled: ye believe in God, believe also in me. Peace I leave with you, my peace I give unto you: not as the world giveth, give I unto you. Let not your heart be troubled, neither let it be afraid." (John 14:1, 27)

Some people seem to have an easier time accepting our Lord's invitation than others. Ray and Sandi Fike are two such people! In *Tell Him With Your Heart,* you will come to know the Fikes as a couple willing to follow the Lord's lead wherever He might take them—from the the rolling hills of New England to the tropical paradise of Hawaii. In times of want and times of plenty, seasons of great pain and seasons of unspeakable joy, Ray and Sandi remained faithful to the Lord's leading and living light, not attached to the things of this world.

In fact, the Fikes live out the Apostle Paul's kind of contentment as purely and surely as anyone I have known.

"for I have learned, in whatsoever state I am, therewith to be content. I know both how to be abased, and I know how to abound: every where and in all things I am instructed both to be full and to be hungry, both to abound and to suffer need. I can do all things through Christ which strengtheneth me." (Philippians 4:11-13)

What's their secret? you ask. That's simple. It's their love of and faith in God and an abiding desire to *tell him with their hearts*.

Let not your heart be troubled!
Scott Stewart

ACKNOWLEDGMENTS

A BOVE ALL THINGS, we would like to thank our Lord for the opportunity to serve Him. We thank the Word of God for revealing the Way, the Truth, and the Life to us by the power of the Holy Spirit.

Words cannot express how much we love and appreciate our Lord. As we look back upon the many pages time has turned, we know that we had to experience many valleys, for without them we would not have seen the beautiful mountaintops of God's glory.

I thank my wife for being the other half of my wings and allowing me to share the love of Christ together as one.

I thank our two miracles of joy God allowed us to nurture and share with in the form of our two special daughters and their families.

I thank the Lord for knitting me together in my mother's womb, walking beside me throughout my life, holding my hand when needed, but most of all for giving His life at Calvary for everyone and allowing me to touch the hem of His garment.

Know that as you partake in our blessed journey, our hearts will be holding hands with you.

INTRODUCTION

TELL *HIM WITH Your Heart* is my meager attempt to share some of the incredible, miraculous moments along life's journey that the Lord has allowed my wife and me to walk, run, and sometimes fall into. But by the mercy of God, we have always risen up on wings as eagles. *Tell Him With Your Heart* is a living testimony that all things really do work together for good to those who love God and whom He calls according to His purpose. It is a story of love—of our special love for each other, of God's love for us, and of our love for Him. It is the story of love between a man and a woman who have become one in Christ. My deepest prayer is that this book will inspire everyone to draw closer to the One who loved us so much that He gave His life—Jesus.

Please do not interpret what I share in this book as in any way prideful or as boasting or searching for praise. All that I do or have done that has any merit to it at all is not through my own power, but through Christ who dwells in me. There is a time and a season for all things that God may be glorified. I pray that our Lord's blessings will be upon you as you embark on the journey recounted in this book. This book provides only a glimpse of the many marvelous things the Lord has done in our life. His mercy is far beyond any measure. Everyone has a story, and our story is one that glorifies God with a testimony of His mercy and grace.

CHAPTER ONE

IN THE VALLEY OF SHADOWS

A
S MY MEMORY drifts back to the spring of 1999, a collage of images appears. Tranquility blends with turmoil. I see many faces with infectious smiles expressing incomparable joy and others with a sad countenance shedding tears that only God could wipe away. This has been true in my own journey.

The sunrise spread a blanket of serenity that seemed to cover me with God's peace. The harmony and beauty set before me gave no indication of the dark clouds that would be on the misty horizon at sunset. The hills and trees cast long shadows and a subtle breeze graced my presence. Then I suddenly remembered that it was time to leave for a routine trip to the VA hospital near Tampa. As I was walking in the back yard of my father-in-law's home before we left, a wild blue jay flew down and perched on my wrist. The bird walked up my arm, stood on my elbow for about two minutes, chirped in its own language, and then flew away. I was unable to interpret his tongue, obviously. After that unusual experience, my wife and I left for the hospital for my routine stress test.

After my 10-minute stroll on a glorified treadmill, they led me down a long hallway for extensive x-rays of my heart. The doctors, nurses, and staff were extremely cordial, which made this uneasy adventure rather pleasant. The test results were inconclusive, and they told me that I needed to have a heart catheterization. Their description of the test did not exactly sound like a good time, but I knew I had to have my heart checked.

Later that day, they placed me under anesthesia for the procedure, which involved running a camera into the main artery where my leg meets my torso and guiding it up and into the arteries of my heart. What they found was both shocking and devastating—especially to me. They told me that four of my arteries were severely blocked. This in itself warranted open-heart surgery, but the worse news was that the two main arteries of my heart were approximately 99% blocked—yes, 99%! They also said that it was possible that I could die at any minute.

Suddenly, my dreams seemed to fade away as dust in the wind. After sharing the grim news with my wife, we decided that we really had no choice but to accept the diagnosis and follow doctor's orders. It was life-or-death, moment by moment. So, standing firm on the promise that God would never forsake us, we prayed in confidence for His guiding hand. After the initial shock dissolved, we sat together and waited for the special cardiac ambulance to arrive. A short while later, I found myself on a stretcher being rolled down a long hallway to an open door that I was not too excited about passing through.

Once outside the door, they placed me in the back of my "medical limo." During the 30-plus-minute drive to the hospital in Tampa, I tried to imagine how everything would ultimately turn out. I could not help but sense the pain my wife, Sandi, must have been going through as I gazed at her from the back of the ambulance. As the love of my life followed us with great sadness on her face, my mind drifted back on a moment when she had been rushed to a hospital. I recalled the many occasions when the Lord had touched my special wife, such as the time God sent His ministering angels to comfort her in extremely trying times. I remembered when He sent an angel to deliver our first daughter, and the miraculous intervention of the Lord during the delivery of our second daughter, when both my wife and daughter literally came back from the dead.

These deeply embedded memories came forth, along with the dozens of other supernatural miracles the Lord had done in our lives. My faith strengthened with assurance that God had already made provisions for this very moment.

At the hospital, they quickly checked me into a room and hooked me up to a labyrinth of tubes. As I looked around, I noticed three other heart patients awaiting their own fate. Suddenly, I felt part of a majority of which I really did not want any association, a member of a "club" that I wanted no part of. (The other three were not as fortunate.)

They scheduled me for open-heart bypass surgery several days in advance. During my prep time, they gave me blood thinners and other medications to prepare my system for this critical event in my life. As I lay in bed, I could not help but reflect on the circumstances that led up to this momentous day. I gazed outside as though I were in a prison serving a life sentence and noticed the sunshine caressing life itself. I found myself trying to be attentive and listen to that still small voice of my big God. Suddenly I realized just how much we take things for grant-ed—things such as the golden sunshine, the kiss of a breeze on our face on a hot summer day, or the smile of contentment on a child's face when a loving parent holds her close. I felt such a deep emptiness when I real-ized I could not do even such a simple thing as embrace my precious wife and ask her if she would like to go for a walk.

At that point, all that was important to me was holding onto the hands of Jesus and praying that He would comfort my dear wife.

The morning before surgery, I had a special time of revival with the Lord. The Spirit of the living God told me to tell the surgeon four things. First and foremost, I was to tell him that a miracle would take place and as a witness to the doctor, God would show him that the hand of God was in control of this operation and that he would have to do only a triple bypass rather than a quadruple.

Second, I was to tell him that this would be the smoothest heart surgery he had performed in the past 20 years. Third, I told him not to fret if I died because God was in control. Finally, I told him not to wire me for a pacemaker because I would not need one and, in fact, two days after the surgery I would be doing so well that they would release me.

After surgery, the doctor confirmed to my wife that all I had told him thus far had come true. I reminded the surgeon that the Lord had personally handpicked him for this delicate surgery. In my quiet time with the Lord just before surgery, the Holy Spirit had whispered the following prophecy in my ear:

"In the shadow of the valley, even the angels know that there is a glorious light. For it is written, one day God's children will be above those who now abide in His presence with continuing adoration. My child, there is no reason to look back and forth, because the presence of the Lord is all you will need to know. For the Lord Himself knows who touches His garment with a faith that cannot be shaken and a love so deeply planted it can cause the dead to waken. Rise up, my child, says the Lord of hosts and life. I have already delivered thee from every curse and strife. In the shadow of the valley, fear no evil; God is with you. I, who was and always will be, hold the keys to death, and I have personally prepared a place for you in due season. I, who still walks among you, and on the third day made a way for everyone... I, who breathes eternal life into your spirit and knew you while formed in utter seclusion... I, who scheduled each day of your life, my child, in the shadow of every valley will be the image and presence of Christ standing by your side."

As tears began to stream down my cheek and the overwhelming compassion of Christ embraced me with a blanket of mercy I will never forget, I felt unworthy to receive such undivided attention. I was so grateful for the many precious moments and the many times that He carried me. Although the doctors could not understand why someone in my condition was not experiencing any pain and were baffled by the fact that I did not have a stroke, it was obvious to me that my Lord was in control. They told me that I passed away twice during surgery. On both occasions, God greeted me with His healing touch.

There is so much more to share concerning my first night in recovery (especially someone's attempt to take my life), but I thank the living God for holding me close. As I briefly reflect on the past few years and think of all the places, miracles, and circumstances that we journeyed through, it is clear to see that the Lord's timing included a high measure of favor and mercy to add to our journey of memories.

I never dreamed that the title of this book would take on such great significance as to prompt me to add another chapter, which would include the physical commitment of open-heart bypass surgery. Even though there were several moments when I was actually near death, and actually died twice, I am thankful that God allowed me more time to share with my precious wife and to walk together for His glory.

When I arrived back at my father-in-law's home to recover only two days after surgery, I went for a short walk (about a mile). Upon returning to the house, I stood outside to quietly reminisce and reflect on what happened before I left for the hospital. As I looked up into the marvelous sky the Lord had set in place that day, I observed a wild blue jay in the distance. He flew down and, as before, landed on my wrist and proceeded to walk up my arm. He stopped at my elbow, looked me in the eye, and chirped for about five minutes. He then flew away and brought back another blue jay that sat on my arm and chirped away. They both flew away and came back a few seconds later with a baby blue jay who also sat on my arm. After this experience, I realized that there was definitely more than just bird talk taking place here. I knew without a doubt that the Lord was assuring me that if He can take care of the birds of the air then He would surely take care of me.

Be blessed in the realization that to live is Christ and to die is gain!

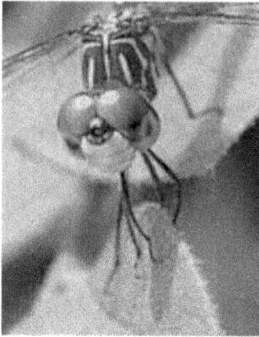

This dragonfly was kind enough to pose for me. I was amazed to see that every dragonfly that I took a picture of that day had a different face.

CHAPTER TWO

THE HEART OF IDENTITY

Proverbs 23:7:
"For as he thinketh in his heart, so is he: Eat and drink, saith he to thee; but his heart is not with thee."

Isaiah 43:2:
"When thou passest through the waters, I will be with thee; and through the rivers, they shall not overflow thee: when thou walkest through the fire, thou shalt not be burned, neither shall the flame kindle upon thee."

Exodus 23:20:
"Behold, I send an angel before thee, to keep thee by the way, and to bring thee into the place, which I have prepared."

I CANNOT EMPHASIZE ENOUGH how relevant these scriptures have been to my own journey through life. From the very beginning, it is evident that the tiny seed that God carefully nurtured had come to fruition by His loving hand. Indeed, it is obvious even to the most skeptical observer how the hand of God supernaturally molded our lives through the years, so that it would blossom into His beauty for His glory. The sad truth is that although we failed the Lord on many occasions, God, in His immeasurable mercy, would reach down to take our hand each time we stumbled. He would lift us up out of the fire and allow us to soar far above life's circumstances.

Born in 1945, I spent my childhood on Cape Cod, Massachusetts. Because my parents divorced before I was born, I often wondered what it would be like to have an earthly father. As I look back, I know my Heavenly Father had a purpose for my circumstance, as He does for all of us. I am not suggesting that God would cause anyone to abandon his family, but rather just acknowledging the fact that God can give meaning and purpose in any situation, no matter how bad it may appear. In my case, these circumstances worked for the better so that I could find my identity in *Christ*. As one deprived of an earthly father, I had a great desire to find and get to know my Heavenly Father.

On the other hand, my precious wife was fortunate to experience a childhood with a loving, caring family whom she adored. My special wife is a full-blooded American Indian, and both her father and grandfather were chiefs in the Iroquois Indian Nation. Her great uncle (Chief Big Tree) posed for the famed American buffalo nickel and appeared in over 60 movies with actors such as John Wayne and many others.

Shortly after my wife and I met, she turned down a professional modeling career. As a teenager, she accepted the position as a New York City Rockettes' dancer. Putting the love of her parents first, however, she gave up the desire of her life to dance and moved back to the reservation in upstate New York.

For the most part, I was content with not knowing my earthly father until the year 1980 when the Lord instilled within my spirit a strong desire to meet him. By this time, I was in my mid-30s, happily married, and had two wonderful daughters. I had a great job with the F.A.A. as an Air Traffic Controller and instructor, and we were living in our dream private estate. Since I had never yet even met my earthly father, I began to wonder about him. *What was he like? Where was he living now after all these years? Did he ever wonder about me?* As questions began to fill my mind, I told my wife that I suddenly had a strong desire to meet him. Not long after my desire reached its peak, the Lord clearly spoke to my spirit, encouraging me to pursue my newfound desire.

For 30 long days, I tried to locate my father, with very little success. Nevertheless, my investigation was not completely fruitless. I was able to locate and speak to many relatives I had never had the opportunity to meet. I found relatives in Pennsylvania, California, Washington, Iowa, Oregon, as well as in other parts of the country. While it was so refreshing to share with them, I found it very strange that none of them had ever heard from my father. After spending a month trying to locate my father, I finally decided to use some wisdom and ask God for help.

When I did, one of the most remarkable things happened—instantly, a telephone number appeared in my mind. Wasting no time, I called the number, a woman answered and immediately blurted out, "I understand that you're looking for your father." *How did she know who I was?* Although a bit stunned by her statement, I quickly came to my senses and replied, "Yes, as a matter of fact I am, do you know where he might be located?"

She told me that I could probably find him in the New Orleans area. After our brief conversation, I hung up the phone and it occurred to me that I had not even asked the woman what her name and address were or how she knew what I was looking for. I then called information in New Orleans, and the operator said that there was no such listing. This was a bit of a setback.

I was in southern New Hampshire, so it was definitely too far to drive, especially since I did not have a specific location and was not even sure my father was living in the New Orleans area. Yet, the question *why would God have given me that number?* persisted in my mind. Not only had God revealed that number to me, but also the woman who answered my call knew exactly why I was calling.

I then asked God for more specifics—in this case, to help me find the correct town. When I opened the map of Louisiana, my eyes focused immediately on the town of La Place. I called the operator and, sure enough, she had a listing for my father.

When I called my father and told him who I was, I immediately sensed his shock.

"Is this some kind of joke?" he asked.

When I explained to him that it was not a joke, he seemed quite stunned. He had put me out of his mind for years, and now when faced with this reality, he had no idea what to say. After I proposed to him that we should meet in person, he hesitated in responding. Mindful of the supernatural circumstances through which I located him, I was determined to meet him. When I persisted in arranging a meeting, he finally agreed.

My wife and I quickly flew down to New Orleans, rented a car, and drove to his address. When we arrived at his home, he seemed happy to see us, but for some inexplicable reason he refused to let us in. Acting in a rather nervous and peculiar fashion, he suggested that we leave his house and go to a nearby restaurant. After arriving at the restaurant, he shared with us the reason he was unable to invite us into his home. After he remarried in 1950, his wife had persuaded him never to call any relatives on his side of the family. Her problem was one of jealousy. She was intensely jealous of his past, and therefore she wanted him to sever all previous relations. This explained why no one ever knew of his whereabouts.

I reassured him that my intention was simply to meet him. Far more, however, came out of our meeting. Before we left, my father handed me a very unusual book. As I glanced at the book and began sifting through the pages, I felt as if I was suddenly in a scene from a movie. In this book was a list of all my relatives back to the year 1751. It also had accounts of many of my relatives who had branched out into other families. According to the book, my descendants were originally from the town of Bernese, located in the Swiss Alps. I also had many relatives in the States who were still living the Amish lifestyle.

It was a blessing to meet my earthly father for the first time, but I soon realized that the relationship I have with my Heavenly Father is far more precious. Nothing can compare with the relationship available to all of us through *Jesus Christ*. He will guide us into all truth whenever we trust in Him. Nevertheless, after this experience it was obvious to me that God also honors the specific desires of our heart, if they fall in line with His will. I had a desire to meet my earthly father, and God fulfilled my desire by revealing my father's whereabouts and giving me more information on my family than I had ever dreamed possible. Remember, all of us go back to Adam and Eve. Several years after that special meeting with my father, I found out that he died, in April of 1995.

Not long after that, my wife and I had the opportunity to travel to Pennsylvania and meet one of my Amish relatives who happened to be in possession of the Fike Family Bible. They had brought this Bible over from Switzerland in 1751, and my great grandfather (seven generations ago) left instructions for it to be in the possession of the closest living relative at the time. After sharing my ancestry with relatives I met for the first time, they were not receptive to giving me the Fike Family Bible. Although I was disappointed, I let the issue go.

It is amazing how time appears to pass more swiftly with age. Even now, events from my early childhood do not seem to be all that far removed from the present. You may find it hard to believe, but I remember events from as far back as when I was six months old, such as the time I felt afraid as my mother would bathe me in the kitchen sink. I believed that if she let me go, I would probably drown. It is puzzling why the mind retains certain memories that appear to be of little importance, while at the same time it discards other memories.

Another memory I recall was from the so-called terrible age of two. At the end of each week, a bakery truck would drive up to our home, and I would beg my mom for pastries. I also remember having feelings of contentment, knowing that it pleased my mother to give me things. God is like that. He enjoys giving His children things that bring us pleasure. To this day, I love doughnuts.

At the age of four, my mother remarried and we moved to Falmouth, Massachusetts. Unfortunately, my mother's new husband could not separate from his family. We had no choice but to move in with his parents. Under the circumstances, I was never able to have a good relationship with my stepfather. As time went by, my mom gave birth to seven other children.

Daily life with my step-grandparents was difficult to say the least. My stepfather and his parents always gave more attention to my brothers and sisters, I suppose because they were of blood relation. At the same time, my stepfather's parents became very jealous and bitter toward both my mother and me. They constantly treated us with contempt, yelling and screaming at us. Not long after we moved in, their acts of animosity escalated. After my stepfather left the house each day for work, his mother would often grab my mom, slap her, even pull her by the hair, and throw her down the stairs. On evenings when my stepfather went out with his friends, his mother would lock my mother and me in the attic.

Nevertheless, despite this unprovoked harsh treatment, those days still produced a few fond memories. During those times when we were locked in the attic, my mother would read me stories to help keep our minds off the situation. In those times, I tried to appear strong, never sharing with my mother the great sadness I felt at her unhappiness. Since they rarely allowed me to eat, I can distinctly remember various nights shortly after 2:00 a.m. when I would sneak downstairs, open the food cabinet, and take a pack of saltine crackers. I would then go outside and find a comfortable first-class seat to sit in and partake in what I visualized was a gourmet dinner under the glorious light of the moon and stars. I was amazed at the seemingly vast array of lights in the sky and often wondered who made it all possible.

For the next eight years, my mother and I continued to receive the same type of unwarranted abuse. Inwardly, I longed to find something to make life a little easier, so I started searching for a father figure to whom I could relate. At the age of seven, I heard about a man named Jim Thorpe, an Indian from Oklahoma. He is in the *Guinness Book of World Records* as the greatest athlete in the history of the United States. Thorpe was the best in everything he did. He was the best in baseball, football, cross-country, track, and, of course, the Olympics. To this day, he holds records in the Olympics that will probably never be broken. Thus, this highly respected athlete became my idol. All I wanted to do in life was to be like him. As a result, I was inspired at the age of seven to start running.

My desire in life at that time was to run my way into the record books. When I was a few years older, I was running up to 10 miles each day. The goal of my intense training was to become the best athlete in all of New England and someday compete in the Olympics.

The underlying reason for these goals was so that my mother could be proud of me. Perhaps my success would take her mind off our dismal family life.

At the age of 12, two dramatic events took place in my life. First, my mother and I moved into the house that my stepfather had finally completed. It felt so great to be free from the torment of my step-grandparents. It was as if we were free from prison.

The other event was not quite so pleasant. One day at the age of 13, I was walking down the street carrying a BB gun when suddenly, out of the corner of my eye, I saw a police car approaching. Startled and a little paranoid, I quickly threw the gun over a fence. After the police officer went by, I jumped over the fence to retrieve my gun. Unfortunately, hidden in the grass near the fence was a broken bottle with a sharp, jagged edge. I jumped over the fence, carefree and unconcerned, as any child would have done. Then, the unthinkable happened. I slipped and landed directly on the broken bottle. The glass entered my kneecap, carving out a small piece of bone in the process. I was in excruciating pain. It is almost as if a pleasant dream had in a single split second turned into a dreadful nightmare. I lay on the ground for about 30 minutes, shocked and confused. My knee stopped bleeding because the tendons hanging from it were blocking the blood's escape route.

I was about a mile from home, yet even short distances like that can seem very long when one cannot even walk. Thus, I began my long journey, crawling along the side of the road in agony, hoping that someone would help me. (No one ever stopped.) As soon as I made it home, I informed my family of the terrible accident. Unfortunately, none of them paid much attention to me, supposing that my accident was not very serious. When I finally got someone to look at my leg, my family still would not take me to the hospital. As I look back on it, I can relate in just a small way to how Jesus must have felt when they drove the nails into His hands and feet.

When I could not walk for several days, my parents finally started to realize that my condition might be more serious than they first thought. As it turned out, it was almost two months before I was able to start walking again. At such a young age, I thought my dreams were shattered and that I would never be able to compete in running. As the months went by, however, I began to run again. I am certain now that it was by the grace and healing power of God that my knee healed up without infection.

After this unfortunate accident, several strange events took place in my life. I recall how one particular beautiful summer night on Cape Cod (when I had reached the "mature" age of 13), I felt led for some reason to go outside and look up at the stars. It was about 11:00 at night, and, as usual, my stepfather was out somewhere and my mother was watching television. The sky was perfectly clear and there was no moon in sight. As I stood in our driveway looking up at the stars, a large flaming object suddenly appeared in the sky. It was round, visually stunning, and pierced the darkness in the brightest color of red I had ever seen. The object was huge, much larger than our house. As I looked on in disbelief, I had the overwhelming sense that it was approaching me at an incredible speed. I would not have time to get out of its way, so at that point I accepted the fact that I was about to die. Fortunately, just before this fiery object was about to hit me, it vanished. Thankful to be alive, I rushed back into the house and told my mother what had happened. Based on her expression, I am not sure she believed me. At times, I am not even sure I believe it myself, yet the experience remains so vivid in my memory even to this day. (It is something I simply cannot explain.)

After that day, I felt inspired to start writing music and poetry. The more I wrote, the more upset my stepfather became. He continually criticized my work and said that I would never get anywhere in life if I wasted my time writing. Without my parents knowing about it, I continued writing and received several contract proposals from various record labels. My stepfather and I did not have any type of genuine relationship at all, and yet this is what led me to seek more of God.

When I was 16, another strange occurrence took place. One night when my mother and stepfather were out for the evening, I remained at home to babysit my brothers and sisters. We were sitting in our living room with the lights out and I was telling stories when suddenly they both seemed disturbed and excited. In unison, they began to tell me that they saw a figure standing in the middle of the room. I could not see anything, so I asked them to describe what they saw. They said the figure was in a long flowing white robe, yet they could not make out what his face looked like. Assuming this was their playful attempt at a prank, I played along with them, even though I did not see anything. I walked over to the center of the room and calmly told the children that I was going to shake this mysterious person's hand.

When I reached out my hand, to my complete surprise, I felt some kind of energy surround it. Then my hand started to get extremely hot. The heat began climbing up my arm. Just before this sensation of extreme heat reached my shoulder, I became so terrified that I pulled away. Immediately, the heat was gone. A bit shaken, I walked back over to the couch and put my hand on my sister's shoulder. She quickly jerked away. When I asked her what was wrong, she told me that it felt like my hand was on fire. It felt okay to me, but apparently to all the others an intense heat was radiating from my hand. After a few minutes, the sensation vanished. That sensation did not return until years later when I touched my future wife's shoulder one day when we were at her parents' home, and the same unexplainable event occurred.

A third incident took place around a year later when I was about 17 years of age. One day while my one-year-old sister was visiting her grandmother, she accidentally pulled a pot of hot coffee off the counter, spilling it all over herself. They rushed her to the hospital and found she had third-degree burns on her arm and chest. Although she received skin grafts over the next several weeks, her skin refused to heal properly. Shortly after this terrible incident, whenever I watched over her, I felt so helpless because I knew she was in pain. One evening after everyone went to bed, I recall glancing at the clock. It was around midnight and I just could not sleep because I was so concerned about my sister. In desperation, I suddenly remembered that someone had told me about a man who healed the sick in *Jesus'* name. With this in mind, I decided to go deep into the woods to be alone and to cry out to God. I said very simply, "God, I know that You can heal, so please heal my sister." Within a few short days after I called on the Lord, my sister's burns seemed to heal up.

As I entered high school, I joined the track and cross-country teams. Our team would eventually become one of the greatest teams in all of New England. In this, I finally achieved one of my goals and became one of the greatest runners in our school's history. Due to our success, my name was in the paper quite often, and that made me feel good because I knew how proud my mother felt.

Nevertheless, there was still another athletic dream that I wanted to fulfill. Each year in Boston, they have a 2½-mile road race in which hundreds of the best runners from all over New England compete. In my last year of high school, I was only one week away from competing in this race. In my eyes this was my chance of a lifetime and would probably ensure a college scholarship. Then, disaster struck.

One morning as I got out of bed, I found that I could not even walk. Apparently, because I had spent so many years running with either cheap footwear or just going barefoot, the arches in my feet had fallen. When I tried to walk, it felt like someone was driving a spike through my ankles. The school I attended felt somewhat responsible, so they took me to a foot specialist. After a thorough examination, the doctor said that in time I would be able to walk if I had special arch supports. He was certain, however, that I would never be able to run again. For some reason, I simply could not accept his diagnosis.

The day of the great race arrived. In order for our team to be eligible to compete, I had to dress up in my uniform and stand on the starting line with my crutches to hold me up. As I stood there waiting for the race to begin, I remember saying quietly, "God, a friend of mine said to me, that in the name of Jesus the sick are healed. If this is true, then I ask you to heal me right now, and I promise that I will run my life for you." The race started, and to my complete astonishment, my legs seemed to have a mind of their own as I started running. About a mile into the race, I realized that I had no pain. In fact, I was not even out of breath. I could barely feel my feet touching the ground. Suddenly, I was overwhelmed with joy as I realized that God had just healed me.

I finished the race in second place. I believe the reason I came in second was simply so God could remind me of His merciful touch and give me the assurance that He would always be first place in my life.

This was certainly a very pivotal day in my life because it gave me an awareness of what God can do when we are willing to believe in Him. The sad thing is that at the age of 19 I was not mature enough in Christ to carry out my promise to God that I would run through life for Him.

At this point, I had just graduated from high school and was considering a career in music as a singer. I had a friend whose father was a millionaire and wanted to manage me. Fortunately, I had enough sense to realize that I was not quite talented enough to make a living as a singer, so I decided to leave home and go into the Air Force.

My first assignment was to attend basic training in San Antonio, Texas. They determined that my career should be in Air Traffic Control. Therefore, after basic training the Air Force sent me to a six-month school in Biloxi, Mississippi.

One evening I decided to go downtown and see what Biloxi had to offer. As I was walking by this large church, some rather unusual noises from inside grabbed my attention, so I decided to enter. There must have been at least 1,000 people inside. Consequently, the only seat I could find was in the back of the church. As the evangelist began speaking about Jesus, I felt drawn to walk up to the altar. As I looked out among the large crowd, I realized that I was the only one who answered the call for salvation. I can truly say, that day I made a firm commitment to Christ.

Nevertheless, the sad truth is that in the years that followed I drifted away from God, the very One who had already done so much for me. I do not know how I could have possibly denied Him after the miraculous works He had already done. God and His mercy would never leave me, however, despite my unfaithfulness.

CHAPTER THREE

ARRANGEMENT BY GOD

Psalm 139:

"O Jehovah, thou hast searched me, and known me.

Thou knowest my downsitting and mine uprising; Thou understandest my thought afar off. Thou searchest out my path and my lying down, and art acquainted with all my ways. For there is not a word in my tongue, but, lo, O Jehovah, thou knowest it altogether. Thou hast beset me behind and before, and laid thy hand upon me.

Such knowledge is too wonderful for me; it is high, I cannot attain unto it. Whither, shall I go from thy Spirit? Or, whither shall I flee from thy presence?

If I ascend up into heaven, thou art there: If I make my bed in Sheol, behold, thou art there. If I take the wings of the morning, and dwell in the uttermost parts of the sea; Even there shall thy hand lead me, and thy right hand shall hold me. If I say, surely, the darkness shall overwhelm me, and the light about me shall be night, Even the darkness hideth not from thee, but the night shineth as the day: The darkness and the light are both alike to thee.

For thou didst form my inward parts, Thou didst cover me in my mother's womb.

I will give thanks unto thee, for I am fearfully, and wonderfully made, wonderful are thy works; and that my soul knoweth right well. My frame was not hidden when I was made in secret, and curiously wrought in the lowest parts of the earth.

Thine eyes did see mine unformed substance; and in thy book they were all written, Even the days that were ordained for me, When as yet there was none of them. How precious also are thy thoughts unto me, O God! How great is the sum of them!

If I should count them, they are more in number than the sand: When I awake, I am still with thee.

Surely thou wilt slay the wicked, O God: Depart from me therefore, ye bloodthirsty men.

For they speak against thee wickedly, and thine enemies take thy name in vain. Do not I hate them? O Jehovah that hate thee, and am not I grieved with those that rise up against thee. I hate them with perfect hatred: They have become mine enemies.

Search me, O God, and know my heart: Try me, and know my thoughts And see if there is any wicked way in me, and lead me in the way everlasting."

I N 1965, WHEN I was 20, an event took place that would change the course of my life forever. At the time, I was still in the Air Force and based at a government command center in Syracuse, New York, as an Air Traffic Controller. One sunny August afternoon, I decided to go into town and visit various stores. When I got downtown, I walked into a very large, exclusive department store. When I passed through the doorway, I noticed from a great distance an extremely attractive young woman. Her appearance struck me like a hammer. In fact, I was quite sure she was the most beautiful young woman I had ever seen. Then, in my spirit, I heard a very clear voice say, "This is the young lady I want you to marry." Unsure what to do at that point, I turned around and immediately walked out of the store and went back to the air base. Upon arrival, I informed my roommate that I had just seen the young woman who was going to be my wife. When I told him that we had not actually met yet, of course he broke down in laughter. I don't blame him. After all, so many people attribute their own desires to a "word from the Almighty."

Nevertheless, there was something genuine about this whole experience. I really believed deep within my heart that this was God's doing. I would never be so presumptuous as to approach her with this knowledge, expecting her to believe me. So I decided that if it really was God's direction, I would not have to pursue this young woman by any natural means whatsoever. God would have to arrange our meeting face to face for the first time when He thought the moment was right. To be quite honest, from an emotional standpoint this was very hard to do because I felt such a strong attraction to this woman whom I had not even met.

I was completely unaware that when I heard that still small voice, Sandi (my wife to be) was going through a very unusual ordeal. It began one day when she was walking to the bus stop on the Indian Reservation to go to work, which was her daily routine. On this particular morning, however, a strange woman pulled up beside her in a car and told her to get in. When Sandi asked what the woman wanted, she said that she had something very important to tell her. A little suspicious, Sandi declined the woman's offer and continued on her way. The woman in the car, however, would not give up so easily. While driving alongside, she began to tell of Sandi's future. She said that in nine months, she would meet a young man whom she would marry soon after, to which Sandi responded: "You're being ridiculous. Please leave me alone."

For the next nine months, though, this woman followed Sandi around and continued to tell her about the future. She would even show up where Sandi worked.

Finally, nine long months later, Sandi had reached her limit. She called her father down to her workplace to tell this strange woman to leave her alone or face legal consequences. When her father began to approach her, the woman started running down the busy main street of Syracuse, New York. Sandi's father finally caught up to her when she came to a stop at a traffic light. When he reached out his hand toward her and grabbed her arm, the woman vanished, disappearing right before his eyes.

Later that same evening, Sandi's friend stopped by her workplace to ask if she would go with her to the USO club where she worked because she had to pick up some items. I had been at the club myself for some time and was about ready to leave when I noticed Sandi walking down the stairs. Again, after nine months, the thought came to me that here was the woman I knew I was going to marry. This had to be God's perfect timing because I rarely went to the USO club. In addition, this was the first time Sandi had ever gone there. What made this event so unusual is that it took place on the same day the mysterious woman vanished.

Without a doubt, this was God's arrangement. On Saturday, May 7, 1966, the love of my life was about to enter my arms. Eight months later, on January 7, 1967, we were married.

Sandi is a full-blooded Native American, a member of the Iroquois tribe in upstate New York. She spent the first 19 years of her life with her family on the Onondaga Indian Reservation in Nedrow, New York. As I shared before, both her father and grandfather were Chiefs on the Reservation, and her great uncle, Chief Big Tree, posed for the famous American Buffalo Nickel.

One day my wife took me to see where her great uncle lived. I was a little surprised to see that he lived in a one-room house with no plumbing, electricity, or modern conveniences. To my surprise, I found out later that he was extremely wealthy and gave all his money away to charity. The reason for his generosity was that he did not want to become like the rich people he knew of and worked with in Hollywood. He said that those who had a lot of material wealth seemed to be caught up in pride, greed, and selfishness. As a result, they were the saddest people he had ever met.

As I look back, I now believe he was right. Perhaps that is exactly why Jesus stated, "It is easier for a camel to go through a needle's eye than for a rich man to enter into God's Kingdom" (Mark 10:25). Not that material wealth is evil of itself, but it becomes evil when we spend all our efforts accumulating it and depending on it as our sole source of security. Due to modern conveniences, most people today do not lean on Christ for their security. They are more secure in the things they can see. This is the complete opposite of what Jesus taught. He emphasized the things we cannot see when He said, "Blessed are those who have not seen, and have believed" (John 20:29). This made a huge impact on my life.

Given the incredible experiences that God had allowed in my life, one might assume that I would be strong in Christ and willing to serve Him with all my heart. Unfortunately, this was not the case. Although I had knowledge of Christ, I still had no sincere inner commitment. I had accepted Him as my Savior, however, the day was coming when my relationship would grow much deeper. Fortunately, God loves us so much that He never leaves us.

My wife was a woman of many talents. She was a professional ballet dancer and teacher and hired to become one of the prestigious Rockettes' dancers in New York City. She was also a licensed beautician, a professional model, and a makeup artist, who graduated from one of the top cosmetic agencies in the country. When she was younger, they chose her to be the Green Corn Dance Indian Princess. She is also a very gifted artist. By far her greatest attribute, however, is that she loves the Lord with all of her heart.

It is now apparent that the Lord had His hand upon Sandi's life from an early age. She was born with a cerebral brain hemorrhage, and the doctors did not expect her to live. Although she did not yet have a relationship with Jesus, God in His tender mercy healed her. Later, as a teenager, she was confined to a bed for almost a year. The doctors were puzzled and did not know what was wrong. Once again, God intervened and healed her.

In 1966, shortly after Sandi and I met, she had a terrible bicycle wreck that left her with an injured Achilles tendon. They rushed her to the hospital. When I learned of the accident, I immediately told her about a ministry that offers prayer 24 hours a day. I told her about my own miraculous healing when I was younger and let her know that I would pray and ask the ministry to pray also. She was walking again in no time.

A few years into our marriage, we decided it was time to have children. The day my wife was about to give birth to our first child, I rushed her to the hospital with great anticipation. After all, this was a very special event for us. Sandi wanted the baby to be perfect in every way, so she chose to have natural childbirth.

As she was lying on the delivery table, the nurse suddenly began shouting for the doctor. The baby, breached in the birth canal, presented a major problem. Immediately, my wife called out to God, and at that moment, a most remarkable thing happened—an angel appeared at the foot of her bed. To the complete dismay of the entire medical staff in attendance, my wife quickly sat up and began to listen to this beautiful celestial messenger.

Of course, Sandi was the only person whom God had allowed to see into the spirit world. While the workers frantically tried to get her to lie down, the angel held her up. God had sent this angel to comfort my wife and see to it that the baby would be born in the normal (head-first) way. The angel told Sandi that God had sent her and that she would turn the baby around right in front of the doctor. The angel also declared that the baby would be born healthy, praising God with her right arm stretching up towards the heavens.

Oddly enough, that is precisely what happened! When the baby was born, she raised her arm straight up in the air. Each time the doctor would put her arm down, our newborn daughter would raise it right back up. Finally, the doctor just left it that way and wrapped her in a blanket. When my wife saw the baby's arm raised heavenward, she then understood what the angel meant when she said that the baby would be born *praising God*.

In November of 1969, the Federal Aviation Administration (FAA) hired me as an Air Traffic Controller. We moved from New York to Oklahoma City, Oklahoma, where I attended the FAA Academy. Several months after I graduated, I put in a request to transfer to New Hampshire. They promised me that I could relocate there in just a few months, but first I had to work at the Chicago Air Traffic Control Center in Aurora, Illinois. After several months in Illinois, I began to grow a little impatient, so I asked again if I could move to New Hampshire. This time, they told me that I could put in for a transfer only after I had been there a few years. Since this was contrary to what they had already promised me, I promptly gave them my notice and quit.

After leaving the Chicago area, we moved back to New York and lived on the Indian Reservation for six months. In September of 1970, my wife and I agreed to move to New Hampshire and start a new life. At the time, we had only $600 to our name. We were really trusting that this was God's direction and that He would work everything out.

Shortly after we arrived in southern New Hampshire, I was able to get a job with a construction company. We moved into a small one-bedroom apartment and for the first three months, we had absolutely no furniture. In fact, we used a cardboard box as our dining room table. After spending most of my money on telephone calls negotiating with the government, they finally re-hired me as an Air Traffic Controller. This miracle was a great blessing. By this time, we desperately needed the money, not to mention the health insurance that would help with the costs of Sandi's pregnancy. At the time, we had no idea of the challenge that was looming directly around the corner. Indeed, we were unaware that no amount of money or medical technology could help preserve the life of our unborn child.

By the time Sandi was finally able to locate a doctor for a check-up, she was six months pregnant. At this point, she wanted to make sure everything was okay with our baby. The news was extremely bad. The doctor performed several tests and concluded that the baby was probably dead—no signs of a heartbeat or any brain waves. He immediately instructed Sandi to go to the hospital to have the baby removed as soon as possible because her life was also at risk. Sandi could not accept the cold finality of the doctor's diagnosis. She absolutely refused to let them abort our baby. She then turned to me and asked me to believe with her that God was going to work everything out.

For three entire months, we stood on our faith in God's power to heal and deliver our daughter safely. There was a brief moment approximately six weeks before our daughter was born when, during a check-up, they tried to move the baby and thought there was a very slight sign that the baby may be alive, but they were not sure. As the projected due date arrived, I took my wife to the hospital not knowing what the future of our second baby would be. The doctors quickly prepared Sandi for surgery. They were actually amazed that she was still alive after carrying what they believed was likely a dead baby in her womb for the preceding three months.

The following is an account of what the nurse in the delivery room told us. Before they began to operate, they did the appropriate tests to see if the baby was likely still dead and confirmed that the baby was indeed still dead. Thus, they prepared for the surgery. At this precise moment, God, in His mercy, brought our daughter back to life. Moreover, the baby's vital signs indicated that she was completely normal.

The medical staff soon began to rejoice over this apparent miracle, until one of the nurses noticed that my wife was not breathing. Surprised by this unexpected turn of events, everyone rushed to attend to her. After an all-out effort to bring my wife back to life, the doctors finally gave up. Although they had exhausted all medical means, they could not revive my precious wife. She was dead. Thank God, however, that the Lord and His mercy once again had the final say. Just when all seemed lost, a Christian nurse in the room started to pray for her, and the monitors began to register marginal signs of life. God intervened miraculously and brought Sandi back.

Thus, we had a double portion of God's miracle power that day. All of these experiences have brought understanding and new light to the following verse in Romans 8:31: "What shall we then say to these things? If God be for us, who can be against us?"

The Lord is my shepherd

CHAPTER FOUR

SEASONS OF MIRACLES

Luke 11:11-13 says,

"If a son shall ask bread of any of you that is a father, will he give him a stone? Or if he asks a fish, will he for a fish give him a serpent? Or if he shall ask an egg, will he offer him a scorpion? If ye then, being evil, know how to give good gifts unto your children: how much more shall your heavenly Father give the Holy Spirit to them that ask him?"

AFTER THE INCREDIBLE miracle of our second daughter, we entered a time in our lives of relative prosperity. In addition to my job at the FAA, I began working in the secular music industry as a promoter. As I mentioned earlier, I had previously been involved in secular music through performing and songwriting--though, as a singer, I never felt I had the talent to go all the way. Nevertheless, given my prior limited knowledge of the music industry I felt as though I could do well as a promoter. Before long, my intuition proved correct and I began taking in a good amount of extra money.

I recall coming home one evening from a concert after midnight. In a blatant attempt to impress my wife, I marched into our bedroom, turned the light on, and dumped $10,000 in cash on top of her. To my surprise, she glanced at me for a second, and then told me to turn out the light and go to bed.

Although it seemed for a moment as though my parade was ending, I realized the truth of the situation. My wife now served Christ, while I was becoming more and more secure in the things of this world. I was allowing myself to grow farther and farther away from the God who had done so much more for me than I deserved. By this time, considering all He had done, I should have been on my knees daily, but sadly that was not the case. Even so, despite my temporary, subtle drift into materialism, God did not give up on me. Quite the opposite in fact, God continued to bless me. In 1973, we bought our first home. The Lord met all of our needs, but I still was not developing a close, vital relationship with Christ. We continued to enjoy all the blessings and security without experiencing genuine spiritual growth and discernment.

1 Peter 2:2-3 says:

"As newborn babes, desire the sincere milk of the word that ye may grow thereby: If so be ye have tasted that the Lord is gracious."

I am ashamed to think how I had tasted God's gracious provision but did not fully desire the spiritual milk of His Word. It is easy to see how God's many blessings lead us to more maturity in Him. Unfortunately, so many of us experience some of His mercy and do not continue to grow by seeking Him out in His Word. The consequences, as I would soon find out, are sometimes quite devastating.

One of those consequences came in the form of meeting a friendly, though rather unusual, lady who would eventually prove to be quite a test. This lady was very interested in Sandi's Indian heritage and desired to find out more about Indian customs and rituals. Furthermore, she sensed some kind of spirituality in both of us. (Later on that would prove to trouble her spirit.)

Unfortunately, as we came to know her a little better, things took a turn for the worse. It was obvious before long that she was a selfproclaimed witch. On top of that, there was even a rumor that she had done the unthinkable and sacrificed two of her children. She admitted that sacrifice was indeed a part of her religion and, unfortunately, was deceived into believing that through reincarnation anyone sacrificed would come back to this world a better person.

One day she took us to the home of a young couple who had recently married. When we arrived at their home, which happened to be one of the oldest houses in town, she suggested that we speak with this couple. Apparently, they were having many strange problems. As we started to pray, I noticed the young lady began to speak in a deep, masculine voice. It did not take long to figure out that she was demon-possessed. Only minutes after we arrived, I witnessed her body and head contort, along with some other unpleasant manifestations. We left their house and heard that several weeks later they were divorced. Soon after, the lady joined a cult and became a witch.

Eventually, our dubious acquaintance tried to persuade us to join her cult, but we were not interested in the least.

2 Corinthians 6:14 says:

"Are ye not unequally yoked together with unbelievers: for what fellowship hath righteousness with unrighteousness? And what communion hath light with darkness?"

It became clear to us that she had some very dangerous beliefs. As we began to explain more about our belief in God, it soon became clear to her that we were not candidates for her witches' coven. Although at first she did not seem to mind the rejection, before long she got angry about our decision and began to make threats against us. She even went so far as to threaten to kidnap our children. As her antagonism began to escalate, her threats soon turned to actions. She actually tried to burn our house down. We warned her that God would take care of us, and in the end, her house burned down instead.

In fact, everything she tried to do against us came back on her. She soon realized a very hard lesson for anyone involved in witchcraft—that our God had more power than she did. Even though we were young in the Lord, we had enough sense to make a rational decision. There is much more to this story I could share, but I do not want to give time to the enemy.

Several years passed and things were still going quite well, at least in a worldly sense. In 1976, God blessed us with our second home, which was the home of our dreams. The way we obtained it proved to be another miracle. The three-story house, built for an executive of the Kellogg Company, was set on several acres of land in Southern New Hampshire. Upon entering the house, we adored the elegant lighting, expensive stylish carpeting, and custom fireplaces. We knew beyond any doubt that *this* was the house for us.

In addition to all the modern furnishings, the house was quite spacious with many rooms to relax in. A winding staircase led up to the bedrooms. The master bedroom had a private bathroom, walk-in closet, and special powder room. When we first took note of the house, it was on the market for a discounted price of approximately $120,000. At the time, I only wanted to spend $70,000. Nevertheless, I was convinced that this was where we were supposed to live.

After I found out that the Merrill Lynch Corporation in New York was the party responsible for the house, I informed the real estate agent that I would deal directly with the corporation, though I assured them that he would receive normal commission. Then, by faith, I informed the corporation that we were going to purchase the house for $70,000 and, beyond that, we needed to move in within three weeks. The real estate agent obviously thought I was crazy, but to his amazement, the corporation accepted my offer and we moved into our private estate within three weeks. Unfortunately, around this time I started to become more materialistic. It is wonderful to have nice things in this life, as long as those *things* do not become the center of your life. By then I was more secure in the things I could see than I was in my God and was beginning to lose a true understanding of who He was.

Shortly after we moved into our dream home, Sandi got very sick and had to go into the hospital. It turned out that she had some major complications and had to have a complete hysterectomy. The only bright spot in this bleak ordeal was that Sandi's roommate turned out to be a local pastor's wife. They quickly became friends, and after the hospital stay, Sandi began attending her friend's church. Sandi tried to get me to go to church, but I just could not seem to make the time for God. I believed that I was in complete control of my destiny and that nothing could possibly go wrong.

In the meantime, Sandi was developing a stronger relationship with Christ, and her first priority was to please Him. As she matured in Christ, He began to reveal certain things to her. My wife was proud of her Indian heritage, but God wanted her to give something up. She had received a small ceremonial mask with the warning that if anything ever happened to the mask, she would die. Now that she was a Christian, Sandi knew that God did not want her to have any idols in her life. Therefore, one day she decided to go to the local dump and dispose of her mask. When she came back from the dump and told me what she had done, I was proud of her. Knowing how she felt about her heritage, I realized what an awesome sacrifice it was for her to rid herself of what many would consider a priceless family heirloom. Her action that day really made an incredible impact on my life. After seeing her great love and commitment for Christ, I started to seek the God who never left me.

During the mid-1970s, the Lord spoke to my wife in an audible voice on several occasions. He would wake my wife up during the night and give her specific scriptures relevant to our situation. As she shared these scriptures with me, I began to see that God truly was who He said He was. In the Word of God, He tells us, "Blessed are those who have not seen, and have believed" (John 20:29).

Unfortunately, 1980 would prove to be another bittersweet chapter in our life. After many years of marriage, my wife's parents separated. Her father left home, and no one knew where he went. Soon after this, however, something rather startling happened. One evening the Lord spoke to my wife in a dream and showed her the exact town, street, and house where her father had moved. The next evening we followed my wife's vision. When we arrived at the location God had shown her, Sandi casually went up and knocked on the door. When her father came to the door and saw his daughter standing there, he stood still with a look of disbelief on his face. That look was unforgettable. After this incident, my faith continued to strengthen daily. All things are possible with the God who knows all things.

As the summer of 1981 began, we had no idea that this was about to become one of the most dramatic years of our life. After 15 years serving as an Air Traffic Controller, I was about to leave my job, which had brought our family financial security for years. The Air Traffic Control strike was set to take place on August 3, and I was not sure what I was going to do afterwards. For the first time in quite a while, I had to trust God for my work situation.

Two weeks before the strike, as we were driving down a road we typically traveled we noticed that a tent revival was taking place. Curious, we decided to stop in for a while and investigate. As I was sitting in the service listening intently, the Lord suddenly and clearly prompted me to go forward. I slowly walked up to the altar. Standing at the altar, I noticed a lot of noise and emotion from a large crowd praising God. Many people came forward for prayer.

I asked God to help me make a decision about whether to leave my secure job or not. Then, suddenly, the Lord shut up my hearing. I was completely deaf to all the noise surrounding me. Although I could see that the people were still talking and moving about, I could not hear anything. Then, as if that were not disturbing enough, God took away my eyesight. At this point, He had my undivided attention. I closed my eyes and, for a split second, I actually feared that when I opened them I would be deaf and blind for the rest of my life. Although I did not really know what was going on, I knew that I was having some type of experience from God and that He wanted my undivided attention.

As I stood there deaf and blind, I noticed that I could no longer physically feel my feet touching the ground. Then, suddenly, it was as if someone was actually standing inside of me pouring hot water all through my system. I could feel the hot liquid flowing through my entire body. The sensation was so soothing that no words can adequately describe it. The next thing I recall is standing in what I believe to be the presence of God. Standing there in awe, all I could see was incredible, unbelievable brightness—so bright in fact that no words in the English language can describe it. Although I could not see anything except brightness, I knew without a doubt that I was in the presence of the King of Kings. I never wanted to leave that moment because it was so soothing. The Lord's perfect peace and brightness embraced me. The rays of His great light seemed to flow through me, and I was convinced that I never wanted to leave that special moment.

After a few minutes, the Lord brought all of my earthly senses back. All I could do was stand there in awe. Through that experience, the Lord spoke to me and encouraged me specifically to give up my job and all that I owned and trust Him to prove Himself faithful to me. He told me that He would provide my every need. When I shared the experience with Sandi, she was elated. She had been waiting for this moment.

That day, we finally became serious about God as a couple, and we seemingly started our life over again as one in Christ.

When the day of the ATC strike arrived, I quit both the union and the government. Before strike day, I personally met with Ronald Reagan. That meeting further encouraged me to make a life-changing decision that day. I also cut all ties with secular music. As I wondered what God had in mind for my life, I went out and started pursuing open doors. I got so desperate that I even went to organizations that were looking for volunteers, but they would not accept me either. Thus, I knew without a doubt that God was in complete control.

Proverbs 3:5-6 says:

"Trust in the Lord *with all thine heart; and lean not unto thine own understanding. In all thy ways acknowledge him, and he shall direct thy paths."*

In 1 Corinthians 6:19, the Lord makes it clear that our body is the temple of the Holy Spirit. Therefore, the closer we walk with God, the more *our* desires actually become *His* desires.

In December of 1981, we decided to take one last vacation—to Hawaii. When we arrived in Honolulu, the weather was warm and beautiful. We felt that in this tropical paradise it would be easy to forget the uncertainty of our future.

Our first Sunday in paradise we attended church. After a beautiful service, a 12-year-old girl came up to us and handed us a small Bible, which contained a strange prophecy, which stated: "We will one day return to paradise." She also mentioned several issues that we had recently gone through, but assured us that God was completely in control and directing our lives. Not thinking much of it at the time, we left paradise in January of 1982 and flew back home to New Hampshire. Our first evening back home, we all sat down by the fireplace praying and pondering, "What now, Lord?"

CHAPTER FIVE

IN THE MASTER'S HANDS

Isaiah 43:2 says:

"When thou passest through the waters, I will be with thee; and through the rivers, they shall not overflow thee: when thou walkest through the fire, thou shalt not be burned; neither shall the flame kindle upon thee."

A FTER WE GOT back from Honolulu, we started our search for work. I heard a rumor that a full-time AM/FM Christian radio station was coming to Southern New Hampshire. Something in my spirit told me that God wanted me to work there. Nevertheless, in order to verify that this was really God, I decided that I would mark on our calendar the exact day on which I felt in my spirit that someone from the radio station would contact me. When that specific day arrived, the telephone rang.

Sure enough, it was someone from the radio station. They promptly invited me to come down to the station to determine whether I could be of assistance. When I got there, the manager informed me that the station was extending its hours to be on the air 24 hours a day. Starting that very day, they needed a DJ between the hours of 11:00 p.m. and 7:00 a.m. I told them that I would gladly take this shift under one condition—that (even though I desperately needed the money) the Lord spoke to me clearly and told me to tell the manager that they were not to pay me any money during the first 90 days of my employment. They refused my offer but immediately gave me the job.

Of course, my sole condition did not seem to disturb them in the least. They accepted my offer, and that night I started working for the first time in over six months. I was on the air 40 hours a week. Since I was not familiar with Christian music, I spent the first three weeks getting acclimated to the various styles and artists.

After three weeks of not saying a word, I decided it was finally time to break out of my shell. One evening I decided that I would turn the music down low, flip the microphone on, and start praying as the Spirit gave me utterance. I was obedient to what I believed the Lord wanted me to do, and as a result, after that moment, my life was never quite the same. As I continued to obey the leading of the Lord, I started to pray on the radio several times each night. In my prayers, I would ask the Lord to bless, heal, and fill those listening with the Holy Spirit. From that moment on, the phone lines would consistently ring throughout the night. I felt a spirit of energy and excitement as God began using me in this new capacity. I remembered reading in God's Word where He said, "He sent His Word and they were healed" (Psalm 107:20). Now I was experiencing the fulfillment of that scripture.

Hundreds of letters came pouring into the radio station as people began sharing their many healings and blessings. Since the station was essentially listener supported, the listeners' responses were very important, and the money was then coming in to meet all of the required needs.

My particular radio broadcast became known as "Faith from the heart." Yet, by all accounts, it was far beyond just a radio broadcast—it was a ministry. Unfortunately, whenever God starts using anyone in this capacity, he can expect opposition. When people are getting their spiritual needs met, the enemy is never pleased. The radio station operated under an interim FCC license, and until the frequency officially sold, the station operated under the control of the current corporation. Since those in charge of the station did not believe in utilizing the gifts of the Spirit, they threatened to let me go if I continued to pray in that manner. This left me in a very uncomfortable situation. Thank God, it was at this time that the Spirit of the Lord spoke to me clearly and told me to continue praying as usual. The Spirit assured me that I would be okay until 15 months later. In the end, this proved to be the Word of the Lord as I was let go exactly 15 months later. Shortly after I left, the station sold.

After the first three months of experiencing the incredible joy that I felt in radio ministry, I began to notice that Sandi and I were unable to spend enough quality time together because I was working all night and she was working all day. Although I enjoyed working at the radio station more than at any job I had ever had in my entire life, I was overlooking the fact that according to the Lord our ministry first begins at home. Knowing how God felt, I was sure in my spirit that this was only for a season.

Ephesians 5:22-28 says:

"Wives, submit yourselves unto your own husbands, as unto the Lord. For the husband is the head of the wife, even as Christ is the head of the church: and he is the saviour of the body. Therefore as the church is subject unto Christ, so let the wives be to their own husbands in every thing. Husbands, love your wives, even as Christ also loved the church, and gave himself for it; That he might sanctify and cleanse it with the washing of water by the word, That he might present it to himself a glorious church, not having spot, or wrinkle, or any such thing; but that it should be holy and without blemish. So ought men to love their wives as their own bodies. He that loveth his wife loveth himself. "

If you do not honor God's Word, then everything else will be out of perspective. 2 Timothy 3:16 proclaims: "All scripture is inspired by God." Even though it was penned by the hands of man, God directed every letter for His purpose and glory. The day after my wife and I found the time to sit down and pray about our situation, the station manager told me I would work the day shift.

This was such a blessing. We were now able to spend time together, but I had to agree not to pray on the radio anymore. I agreed, but God still moved in mighty ways. Instead of praying as usual, I would give a scripture before each song as the Spirit led me. No one could argue with reading a scripture on a Christian radio station.

One of the many miracles that took place happened on my very last night of working the midnight shift. I asked the Lord to do something special as a confirmation that I was in His perfect will. I said, "Lord, since tonight is my last night to pray on Christian radio, I ask you in the name of Jesus to fill this radio station with your holy angels and stand by my side to inspire and direct the words that I should say. Then, I ask you to show one of the listeners this vision and have them call me to confirm it."

On the surface, such a prayer might seem a little unusual and perhaps immature. At this point, I would be more inclined to agree with that assessment; however, remember that the Lord wants us to come to Him with a sincere heart as a child. Remember also that at this time I was a new Christian with an incredible zeal to please God. Sadly, on various occasions I have seen many Christians who think they have wisdom beyond compare. It is almost as if these people believed they no longer have to seek God's advice for anything. That is absurd, of course. After I prayed that night, to my surprise, the phones did not ring at all. I wondered if I had somehow offended God in some manner. Usually the phones would be ringing off the hook.

The entire night passed before the phone finally rang, at 6:00 a.m. The woman on the other end announced that she was calling from the

Boston area. In a state of extreme excitement, she proceeded to tell me about her supernatural experience. She said that while I was praying, she had a vision in which she saw me sitting in front of the microphone praying. She said the station was full of angels, and that one of the angels standing beside me appeared to be feeding me something as I was praying. Upon hearing this, I almost fell out of my chair. Not only did she describe everything that I had asked the Lord for, but she also said that this was the first time that she had ever had a vision or seen angels. She went on to tell me that for years she had a problem with her back, but during our prayer of agreement she felt the hand of God touch her, leaving her completely healed.

Although many miracles took place during my blessed time on the air, this one was very special. After all these years, I still have that letter stored in a safe to remind me of all those special times the Lord allowed me to minister His presence. I certainly was not worthy of such a blessed time.

By this time, I had developed quite a rapport with the various church denominations and organizations in the area. As a result, when the need arose to sell commercial spots, the door opened for me to become a sales manager. Eventually, I would wear many hats at the radio station—Public Relations Director, Commercial Writer, Advertising Director, full-time DJ, Concert Director, Activity Director, Fund Coordinator, and even Sales Manager. I left the radio station in June of 1983. Sandi was the secretary at the radio station and was also let go. We were once again in a position to seek and wait on the Lord for direction concerning jobs.

Not long after this blessed time, Sandi began feeling very sick and went to see a doctor. After taking numerous x-rays and blood tests, the doctor informed us that the news was not good. A tumor showed up on the x-ray, and the subsequent blood tests indicated that she had cancer. Apparently, the cancer had already spread throughout her system. The infection caused the ends of all of her fingers to swell to about twice their normal size. Of course, this was devastating to both of us. They scheduled Sandi for surgery the next week for two procedures—one to remove the cancerous tumor and another to possibly remove her fingernails.

When the day of surgery arrived, we prayed before they began preparing Sandi for the procedures. The doctors decided to complete another round of x-rays and blood tests. To their amazement, the tumor had vanished, her blood tests were clear, and the growth on the end of her fingers just fell off. We were immediately thankful to God for once again coming through for us in such a miraculous way. We were convinced more than ever that God had some special plans for both of us. Throughout that year, God continued to shower His blessings and healing power over both of us.

About a year later, Sandi once again became very ill. One evening as she lay on the bed, her fever shot up to 104 degrees and she began to fade in and out of consciousness. We rushed to the doctor's office, but by the time we got there, her temperature had returned to normal. I found this very strange, especially when it happened on two other occasions. In my heart, I sensed that we were dealing with spiritual forces, and thus I became very concerned. That is not to say that I became fearful or worried. There is a fine line between worry and concern.

One evening after Sandi's fever again rose to 104 degrees, I knew it was useless to take her to the doctor because of what had happened on the three previous occasions. So, instead, I sincerely prayed to God for an answer to this strange illness. Soon afterwards, I felt an incredible peace deep within my heart as the Spirit revealed to me exactly how I should pray. Many Christians mistakenly think that *how* we pray is unimportant so long as we pray. Nothing could be further from the truth. Excited by the attentive word from the Lord, I took Sandi up to bed knowing in confidence that the Lord was about to perform another incredible miracle. I started to pray as the Lord had directed me when, suddenly, I could see through the eyes of my wife and into the spirit world.

Something very unusual happened then. Sandi thought she saw me get up and leave the room, leaving her all alone. This was just a trick of the enemy, however. In reality, I never left my wife's side. As I continued to pray for her, a demonic figure suddenly appeared in front of her. Even with my eyes closed, I could see this figure in the spirit realm. It was short and very animal-like in appearance. As it stood in front of her, I noticed it was laughing at her as she lay there in extreme pain. I tried to ignore the demon and just continued praying as the Lord directed me. Then I experienced an incredible feeling of confidence. I could sense in my spirit that something miraculous was about to occur. As the room filled with angels, I knew that God was answering my prayer and was about to touch my wife in a special way. The demon quickly left in agony, and Sandi's fever was gone. She then spent the next hour dancing and singing in the Spirit with the angels who were in the room. I know that sounds hard to believe, but I was there.

The following morning Sandi seemed fine, so I went to work. During that day, one of Sandi's friends came by the house for a visit. When Sandi's fever once again rose to about 104 degrees, her friend rushed her to the hospital. As soon as I found out that Sandi was at the hospital, I rushed there to see how she was. I was very surprised, of course, because I felt that the prayers the night before had taken care of this problem.

It just so happened that the doctor who was to take care of her was the same one who had witnessed the miraculous healing of her cancer. After running several tests, he diagnosed her with a severe case of hepatitis and said she could expect to spend up to a month in the hospital. Sandi then said something rather unusual. She informed the doctor with total confidence that just as Jesus rose on the third day, three days from then she would also arise from her bed completely healed and ready to go home. The doctor's response was that he could not explain her healing from cancer. Sandi reminded the doctor that the blood of Jesus cleanses all. On the third day, the Lord once again showed this doctor a mighty miracle. When there were no signs she had ever had hepatitis, he had no choice but to release her from the hospital and allow her to return home.

After these two miraculous healings, I received a special song from the Lord. The song, titled "Tell Him with Your Heart," is about Christ, who loved us so much that He gave His whole heart and life for all humankind. The words and melody came to me instantly, as if I had just turned on the radio. His desire is that we come to Him with that same attitude. Unfortunately, we Christians are sometimes embarrassed to admit that we even know the Lord. It often depends on whom we are with, what we are doing, and what we think we might gain or lose. *Tell Him with your heart* means to give yourself completely to God, all the time, in every situation, and to love and obey all His commandments so that He will be glorified.

Shortly after I wrote this song under the inspiration of the Holy Spirit, Sandi went on a retreat in Vermont. Although she did not know anyone there, she went to be refreshed and to hear from the Lord. While she was there praying with a group of women, one of the women started singing. As Sandi listened, she could not believe what she was hearing. A woman in the group had begun to sing the words and melody of the song that I had just finished writing—"Tell Him with Your Heart." Afterwards, my wife asked the woman how she knew that song.

The woman responded, "This is a confirmation from the Lord that He has His hand upon you and your husband." Then the woman sang another song.

Sandi said the next song was also very beautiful, but she had never heard it. When she asked the lady what the song was that she had just sung, the lady replied, "The Lord says that from this day forward, no one here will remember the words or the melody of this song; but in due season this song will be given to your husband, and it will be known nationwide for God's glory." What an incredible prophetic blessing!

One summer day in 1982, I left for work knowing that the bank was coming to foreclose on our dream home. Despite the disturbing nature of this news, I had perfect peace about the situation.

That morning as Sandi sat alone in our living room with tears rolling down her face, she cried out to God for help in this critical situation. God sent a host of Heavenly Angels to minister to Sandi. They assured her that everything was going to be fine. They revealed to her that we were not going to leave our home because it was not yet time. Then, finally, that dreadful knock on the door radiated throughout the house. Sandi answered the door and, sure enough, it was the officials from the bank.

Upon entering, they wasted no time in delivering some unbelievable news. They said that even though they were taking over the house, they would allow our family to stay there free of charge until house sold. Thus, it was easy for us to recognize God's hand in this matter. Sandi gladly agreed and they left.

As amazing as it may seem, during the next full year no one ever called or came out to look at the house. This is just another testimony of how God can take a bad situation and turn it completely around. Not only did we still have a place to live, we lived there rent-free. Naturally, I have to give God all the glory in this matter.

After another year passed, we received a phone call from the bank. They informed us that they had recently sold the mortgage to another company. We were then responsible for negotiating an arrangement with the new owners.

We drove downtown to meet with the new mortgage company, but before we went inside, we decided that we should pray and ask God for His help and guidance. In our prayer, we told the Lord that all we could afford for rent was $350 per month. The mortgage officer greeted us and invited us to his office. He got right to the point and told us that we had to either move out within 30 days or agree to pay a monthly rental fee of $1000. I told him that it was our desire to stay in the house until it sold, but we simply could not afford that much money. The room fell silent, and I felt led to ask him to consult with his boss once again and see if there was some way we could stay in the house for less rent. He left the office for a very long five minutes. When he returned, he said that we could stay in the house for $350 per month until the house sold. Once again, God came through and met us precisely at the point of our faith.

Another year went by during which no one ever came to look at the house. It was so comforting to realize that God was the One who really held our mortgage. Again, a year later, when it was time to renegotiate our payments, we felt that it was finally time to let go of the house, as we had perfect peace about the decision. We informed the mortgage company of our intentions and gave them a date when we would vacate the property.

The night before we were to leave the property, we still did not have a place to move. Late that evening some friends dropped by unexpectedly to say hello. They told us that they were going on vacation for two weeks and just wanted to say goodbye and see how we were doing. God led them to stop by our home that night. When we told them of our situation, they said without any hesitation that we could stay at their house while they were on vacation. Not only was that an incredible blessing, but someone else knew a place where we could store our furniture and agreed to pick it up.

The next day we moved as scheduled. That same afternoon, we met a couple who lived down the street from where we were staying, and it just so happened that they were about to move out of their duplex. They asked us if we were interested in renting it, and we told them yes. The owner accepted our offer and we move in a short while later.

The Lord was more than gracious to me after I gave my heart to Him and made the choice to give up my materialistic lifestyle back in 1981. Over the years that followed, the Lord opened doors for numerous job positions. These included sales manager for a Christian radio station, manager for a large construction company, manager of a water well-drilling company, order administrator for a major computer company, and manager of a sign company. I also obtained a real estate license in New England, worked in New York as a property manager for a private estate, and obtained a license in the state of Florida for condominium management. I obtained a license and was ordained under the ministry of New England Pentecostal Churches, was Advertising Director and Concert Promoter for several churches in New England, a Consultant for East Agency Concerts of Boston, and during the period from 1982 to 1990, I had my own Concert Promotion Company called "Loving Heart Ministries."

When I gave up my deep involvement in secular music, the Lord gave me the desire of my heart by allowing me to work in Christian music, and I praise Him for that. As a promoter, I had the opportunity to work with such artists as Larnelle Harris, Twila Paris, Scott Wesley Brown, Amy Grant, Mike Adkins, and Kathy Troccoli. I also worked with Wayne Watson, Kelly Willard, Paul and Rita Baloche, Phil Nash, Dick Tunney, Michelle Pillar, Kim Boyce, Michael W. Smith, Gary Chapman, Sandi Patti, Dallas Holm, Ian & Annie, Bob Thompson, Randy Coryell, Phil Driscoll, Steven Curtis Chapman, and many others. I must also mention what a privilege it is to know many other artists, such as Andy Chrisman of Church on the Move in Tulsa, Oklahoma (he is a true man of God, gifted, and extremely attentive to the voice of our Lord). If you are ever in Tulsa, make sure you visit.

I am also thankful for my dear talented friend Dino Kartsonakis who certainly brings glory to our God, as he has performed and ministered in over 200 countries. (WOW!) That is an incredible feat. All that I have done or accomplished that has any significance to it at all was not in my own power but by the hand and inspiration of God. If you trust in God, He will open doors that no man can shut.

I could share so many stories about the special times that I was able to enjoy with many of the aforementioned Christian artists. Nevertheless, I feel led to share about someone who is also very special to our heart, Twila Paris. We have known her since she stayed at our dream estate in

New Hampshire back in 1983. One day, after a New England tour, she suddenly turned around to give us something. To our complete surprise, she handed us a personal check for the same amount of money that I had paid her that weekend. She told us to donate it to our church. She has such a tender heart.

CHAPTER SIX

HE WILL NEVER LEAVE YOU

Isaiah 59:19 says:

"They shall fear the name of the Lord from the west, and His glory from the rising of the sun. When the enemy shall come in like a flood, the Spirit of the Lord shall lift up a standard against him."

THE TRUTH IS, if God is for us, then who can possibly be against us. His name is above all names, and if you have not yet developed that intimate relationship with Him, let me encourage you to seek and you will find, knock and He will open up the door. He will prove His Word to you if you are willing to trust Him.

I recall a day in 1989 that became yet another opportunity for God to perform a miracle. Sandi went to have lunch with our daughter. Afterwards, her goodbye could very well have been her last. As she drove away from the restaurant, she came to an intersection. As she started to make a left turn, a truck ran a red light and barreled straight toward her from the opposite direction. In a split second, the approaching truck smashed into her. As fuel was gushing out of the gas tank, those who had witnessed the accident began screaming for Sandi to get out of her car before it burst into flames. When she tried to get out of the car, her legs refused to budge.

When the rescue squad arrived, they had to cut the car open to get her out and then rushed her to the hospital. When I got the call, I left work and headed for the hospital in a state of disbelief. At the time, I had no clue as to the extent of her injuries. Of course, the devil wasted no time in filling my mind with images of my wife lying in the hospital lifeless. When I arrived at the hospital, they immediately took me into the emergency room. When I walked up to Sandi's bed, she saw me and started to cry. I asked her what had happened and the first thing she said was, "I'm sorry I destroyed the car."

Despite this serious situation, I was slightly amused at her comment. I told her that I couldn't care less about the car; I just wanted to know how she was. We held hands and started to pray together, and within the hour, our God touched her with healing. Not long after, we walked out of the hospital, holding hands and praising God for His healing touch.

We were about to find out that 1989 would become a year that we would not soon forget.

During that summer, our daughter Patty was able to fulfill one of her life-long dreams. She went to Tulsa, Oklahoma, to attend Oral Roberts University and eventually received her degree in journalism. When we left Patty at school and flew back to New Hampshire, we experienced the "empty nest syndrome." I suppose we never truly realized how much pain this would bring.

Several weeks later, Patty called us one night after midnight. We would not soon forget this phone call. When I picked up the phone, I heard someone crying. Right away, the voice on the other end cried out, "This is Patty; you have to help me, help me, please."

She was in a state of panic, so I asked her what was wrong. Suddenly, the phone went silent.

You can imagine how Sandi and I felt. It was about 1:00 a.m. and our daughter did not even have a telephone in her room; we did not know who to call or what to do. A few minutes later, Patty called back. She kept yelling, "You have to help me! You have to help me!"

When I asked her where she was, she said she didn't know and continued to call out for help. Once again, the phone line went dead. After trying for over an hour, we were finally able to reach someone at ORU. We told him what had happened. They immediately went to Patty's dorm room to check on her. When they went to her room, they found Patty fast asleep. In fact, she had never left her room that evening, and since she did not have a phone in her room, she could not possibly have called us. Evidently, the enemy was so anxious to cause panic and strife in our life that he actually arranged a phone call just to draw us into fear and confusion.

After this incident, we knew without a doubt that Patty was right where God wanted her to be.

In 1989, Sandi received another special blessing. One day when she was visiting a beauty salon, the owner turned over the entire business to her and told her she could do whatever she wanted with it. My wife was speechless. She soon reopened the salon under the name of *Heaven Sent*, since the hand of the Lord gave it to her. At the beauty shop, my wife would hold weekly Bible studies. The Bible studies were a blessing, and business was flourishing. After about a year, Sandi gave the entire business to another Christian in order to bless and meet her need.

After Sandi gave the business away, she established a ministry to those in need of a beautician. She would go to hospitals and nursing homes and offer her services as a beautician free of charge to those who were in need and could not afford it. She received great joy from doing this, and the Lord opened up many opportunities for her to witness. Because of her work, I too got involved, and even ministered to entire wards in various hospitals and nursing homes. What a blessing to help bring a smile to the face of those who had little or no hope. During this time of ministry, we thank God that many came to know the Lord.

One time, someone asked Sandi to come to the nursing home to do the hair of a woman who was in a comatose state and very near death. As my wife was doing her hair, we felt led to share the message of salvation and pray for her despite her complete lack of awareness. The next day we found out that she had died shortly after we left. Afterwards, the woman's husband called my wife to thank her for doing his wife's hair. He wanted to share something else with us, something very important. He told us that just before his wife died, she came out of her coma and said, "Don't worry about me. Earlier today, my beautician and her husband told me where I was going and led me to Christ." With that, she smiled and went on to be with the Lord in Paradise.

From this experience, I realize that we must never think that it is *ever* too late to share the Gospel with or witness to anyone, even if they are in a coma. As long as they hang on to life, we can always minister Christ to them.

I remember another elderly woman Sandi was able to help. One day this woman called and asked Sandi to come over to her house and do her hair. That afternoon, while Sandi was doing her hair, the woman sadly informed her: "I probably won't see you again." She then began to tell Sandi that she appreciated the many times that she was willing to come over and help her and especially appreciated those special times when she talked about Jesus. After Sandi finished doing her hair that day, the woman called her daughter into the room and said, "If anything ever happens to me, I want my car to go to Sandi." A few hours later the woman died.

The next day Sandi received a phone call from one of the woman's relatives who asked her to come over to the house. When she arrived at the house, they took her to the garage and opened the door. Sandi was in awe to find a custom Jaguar in mint condition parked in the garage. Unfortunately, one of the relatives visiting from out of town began to cause a scene, demanding that the car was hers. It is amazing how often relatives will fight over possessions, sometimes even before a person has passed away. Although the other relatives explained that their mother specifically said that this car was to go to my wife, Sandi told them that she was not there to fight over material possessions. She was there because she cared about the woman. She told them to keep the car in their family; it was the thought that was important, not the car.

In Matthew 5:40-42 , Jesus said:

> *"And if any man will sue thee at the law, and take away thy coat, let him have thy cloak also. And whosoever shall compel thee to go a mile, go with him twain. Give to him that asketh thee, and from him that would borrow of thee turn not thou away."*

Even though Sandi had a legal right to the car, it would not have been a good witness for her to force her right on the family. We thank God for yet another opportunity to prove His work in us.

One of the last things that happened during our blessed time in New Hampshire involved a very close friend. She had a 20-year-old son named Darren, who swerved off the road and crashed his car into a tree. At the hospital, they discovered that he had sustained severe brain damage and internal bleeding. His mother immediately called us, sobbing, and informed us of his condition. She let us know that the doctors did not expect him to live through the night. She explained that, even if he did live, he would probably be in a vegetative state for the rest of his life.

We rushed to the hospital and quickly found our friend and prayed with her. Soon after, Sandi and I went to the room to pray for Darren. As soon as we started praying, the Spirit came upon Sandi in an unusual manner. God revealed to her exactly what to pray in an unknown language, for which she also received the interpretation. As we were praying, the medical staff came back into the room. As we looked on, blood began to pour from Darren's nose, but as we continued to pray, the bleeding stopped completely.

Over the next few days, Darren made a miraculous recovery. After a brief stay in rehab, they discharged him. We were so happy when he informed us that he was on his way to attend Bible school. God had performed yet another incredible miracle.

CHAPTER SEVEN

LOST IN PARADISE

W HEN 1990 ROLLED around, we were still living in New England. God had blessed us with the opportunity to live in that area for 20 years and make many beautiful memories that we will cherish forever. Nevertheless, it was time for God once again to take our hands and lead us down the path He had ordained for us to follow even from the foundation of the world. He allowed us to experience both the valleys and the mountaintops for His glorification. After spending several days in prayer, Sandi and I knew in confidence that God was about to open a new door in our lives. By the way, between 1967 through 2015, we have moved 70 times.

In the spring of that same year, I received a call from a former real estate associate calling from Hawaii with a job offer. To my astonishment, he asked me if I would consider a position as assistant vice president for a corporation that had just secured $3.1 billion worth of land acquisitions in American Samoa. Equipped with excellent properties and virtually unlimited resources, their intention was to build the number-one resort in the entire world.

After the initial surprise faded, I calmly told him that I was interested. I asked him what my job description would be. He explained some of the responsibilities as well as the benefits of the job in Honolulu, Hawaii. I would be required to contact the CEO of the company in American Samoa at least once each week to update him on the progress of developing and securing both the staff and corporations that would be responsible for building the resort. Since the CEO of the corporation was a pilot, I would have the authority to set the stage for negotiations to purchase Donald Trump's executive jet. I would have the authority to locate and preview the most expensive estates on the island of Oahu. These estates were valued between $5,000,000–40,000,000, and I was to find the best one available for the corporate headquarters. I would also be responsible for hiring the entire staff for this project. In addition, he said that I would receive a salary of approximately $250,000 the first year along with substantial benefits. By the second year, he assured me that I would be a millionaire.

Of course, all this seemed quite overwhelming. But I was now secure in the things of God and open to what He had in store for us. As I began to consider this remarkable opportunity, my mind wandered back to a previous time when we were in Hawaii. Something very peculiar had happened. On vacation in 1981, we had decided to attend a particular church. After the service, the only person who came up to greet us was a young girl who walked up and handed me a small Bible. I didn't think much of it at the time, but when I opened the Bible sometime later, I was amazed to discover that the young girl had written a very specific prophecy on the inside cover concerning my wife and me. She was right on target about a number of things that had already happened, and she concluded the prophecy with a word that stated, "Someday God will bring you back to Hawaii." After further consideration, we eventually accepted this prior prophetic word as confirmation. Consequently, I made the decision in my heart that this was what the Lord wanted us to do.

We experienced the fulfillment of prophecy. Before we left New Hampshire, God directed us to give up all that we owned to a specific church where we worshipped. We felt this was a privilege because we knew it would help meet the needs of others and that, as a result, God would bless us. We will always be grateful to our pastor and close friend for his kindness because he also blessed us.

So then, there was no turning back. We were finally on our way to Hawaii to begin our new life in paradise. We had no foreknowledge of the strange test that was looming on the horizon. Fortunately, God knew everything, and He had His hand on our lives to fulfill His purpose for His glory.

Shortly after arriving in Hawaii, our lifestyle underwent a rapid transformation. We immediately received a rental car and a luxury hotel suite, and we went shopping to purchase some new wardrobes that would meet the demands of doing business among the upper echelons of society in this warm and beautiful "tropical paradise." As I proceeded to fulfill my job responsibilities, I was amazed at how people responded to me. Just by saying who I was and what I represented, I was able to contact and speak to virtually anyone in the world. With a few words of introduction, I found doors flying open and the red carpet rolled out at every turn. Of course, I attributed this success to the favor of God. I admit that Sandi and I really enjoyed this change of pace.

Perhaps our most interesting assignment was choosing an estate as headquarters. We were anxious to undertake the grueling task of visiting the most elegant estates in Hawaii. Paul Mitchell, who made his fortune from haircare products, built one of the estates we visited. This estate, with its waterfalls and priceless woodwork, was valued at over $20,000,000. Another enormous beachfront estate was valued at $40,000,000. The luxurious layout of these houses was astonishing. It was as though God allowed us a very small glimpse of the beautiful architecture that awaits God's children in Heaven.

Because of the decisions we were empowered to make, we often became the center of attention. The real estate agents would take us to the finest restaurants on the island in their flagrant attempt to persuade us to purchase one of their properties. I was careful, however, not to allow our newfound prosperity to erode the principles that God had taught me in the past. Many times while dining at these establishments, I would observe some of the so-called "elite" of this world. Delivered many years prior from materialism, these experiences especially reminded me of some of those lessons I had learned, I knew that God was not a respecter of persons and that chasing after material wealth and worldly pleasure was a dead-end. From that time on, I had learned to seek first the kingdom of God, and I knew He who would supply all my needs according to His will and purpose. The time had come to put those principles to the test. The fact is, many people do not realize how much of a test prosperity actually is. It is easy to see how important it was that we did not allow this new lifestyle to choke out God's work in our lives. Had we allowed ourselves to be taken in and ensnared, we would have never survived the drastic changes soon to come.

In paradise, Sandi and I enjoyed many times of relaxation. At least once each day we would take a peaceful stroll along the beach. Even now as I look back, those peaceful moments were such a blessing from the Lord. In fact, it seems rather strange that some of the fondest memories of those days were not of a luxurious lifestyle but rather of quality time in the company of my wife, enjoying the sights and sounds of God's handiwork.

It is difficult to understand the expression "the best things in life are free" until one has experienced firsthand some of the best things money can buy. The things money can buy, however, are temporary, and as we would soon find out circumstances can change at any time. Fortunately, God in His mercy knew and scheduled many precious moments, moments that Sandi and I can look back on with joy.

As time drifted by, things seemed to go quite well until one day a single phone call turned our world upside down. On Christmas Eve 1990, my partner called me at our hotel suite and informed me that he was at the airport boarding a plane to Osaka, Japan. He went on to explain that he had recently closed down the company and all of its bank accounts. Suddenly, with only a brief phone call to serve notice, I was officially out of a job. Since he had access to all my finances, I soon found out I was in a very serious condition. I told Sandi that the company had closed, along with all of our bank and credit card accounts. All I had to my name was $10. Furthermore, in one week we would have to return our rental car and leave the keys to our hotel suite at the desk.

On the one hand, I was of course devastated. On the other hand, however, we had been through so much before that deep down inside I was sure God was still in control. I did not have the right to harbor bitterness and resentment toward those responsible for this outrageous twist of events.

During our last week at the hotel, we aggressively pursued employment, but God closed every door. I am quite sure it was God because there were many job opportunities in Honolulu. Solemnly, I said to my wife, "I believe that we are truly 'lost in paradise.'"

Between the two of us, we had only one airline ticket to New York. I told Sandi to go and stay with her mother, and I would eventually find a way out of paradise. At this point, Sandi reminded me that we were one in Christ and then proceeded to rip up the ticket and give me a hug.

My wife declared reassuringly, "God will take care of us because that is His promise."

There were HELP WANTED signs everywhere in shops and businesses. The signs seemed to mock me. I felt like making my own HELP WANTED sign and holding it up to God to remind Him of our condition. Yet, God knows all things. I was simply in the process of learning that God sometimes allows us to experience what seems to be a disaster to show us that all we need to do is trust in Him. The verse "trust in the

Lord with all your heart and lean not to your own understanding, and He will direct your paths" (Proverbs 3:5-6) would never be meaningful without an excellent opportunity such as this to really trust Him. Indeed, we had no choice but to trust Him. In addition, somewhere deep inside, I began to believe that all things do work together for the good of those who love God and are called according to His purpose.

The next Monday, a loud pounding on the pavement outside the hotel awakened us rather abruptly at 6:00 a.m. Apparently, in order for some of the street people to obtain money, each morning they would gather empty cans and crush them so they could fit large quantities into bags to sell. The enemy tried to use this as a dark reminder to draw us into fear. I thought to myself, *Am I going to be pounding cans for a living?* Then Satan filled my head with images of Sandi and me lying beside the rocks on Waikiki Beach among other homeless beggars. I had previously observed many people in this condition and could not believe that God would allow this to happen to us.

The dreaded hour of 9:00 a.m. quickly arrived: checkout time. We had to leave the comfort and security of our suite and proceed down the winding path to Waikiki Beach and an uncertain fate. With our suitcases packed, I walked over to the door and turned the doorknob. At that precise moment, the telephone rang. Thoughts began racing through my mind. I anxiously put down our luggage, thinking, *Is it possible that God is going to intervene and rescue us from this impending disaster?* With an array of thoughts bubbling up inside of me, I picked up the phone.

On the other end a vaguely familiar voice said, "Hello, Ray, this is John." John was a young man I had met three months earlier at a church service we attended. When we met, I shared a small portion of our testimony with him and told him where we were staying and what we were doing. His call surprised me. John immediately informed me that neither he nor his wife could sleep the previous night and that the Lord strongly impressed upon them to call us. John had never called me before.

When I explained what had happened, John told me to meet him outside our hotel in 30 minutes. If John and his wife had not attended to that still small voice of the Lord, the entire course of our lives might have changed that day. This is why fellowship with others is so important because many times God uses people to fulfill His purpose. *None of us has it all together, but all of us together have it all.*

John and his wife arrived outside our hotel in two vehicles. He handed me a set of keys to one of them and said, "This is your car, free of charge, as long as you need it." Then he handed me another set of keys with a note that read, "This is where we live; go and make yourself at home." Before they left, they said they would be home later that evening and had already prepared a room for us.

Completely stunned, I turned to Sandi and said, "This is incredible." This couple did not know us at all and yet trusted us completely with their car and their home. Thanks to God's providing hand and John's obedience, though, we had transportation and a place to live. I recalled God's Word that states, "I go to prepare a place for you. And if I go and prepare a place for you, I will come again, and receive you unto myself; that where I am, there ye may be also.... I will not leave you comfortless: I will come to you" (John 14:2-3, 18).

Obviously, this scripture applies to our eternal home someday, but it is so reassuring to know that you can count on God for all things even here and now. Although He does not always answer the way we would like him to, He is and always will be God. The only thing we needed then was a job, food, and some money. I knew that the same God who provided transportation and housing would surely meet the rest of our needs.

That evening when John and his wife, Susan, arrived home, it was not long before we experienced a clash of cultures. They invited us to eat with them, and immediately Susan went to the kitchen and started to make dinner. Hungry, and a bit curious, I walked into the kitchen to see what she was cooking. As I looked on the stove, I could not believe my eyes. In one pot, chicken feet swirled around in the boiling water. In another pot, I observed what appeared to be fish eyes staring back at me. With an apologetic tone, and a very queasy stomach, I explained to Susan that we just could not eat that type of food. Fortunately, she understood and cooked us some rice.

John and Susan had two children, and despite our different tastes in cuisine, we got along with him and his family quite well. John was African-American and his wife was Chinese. Consequently, their children were dark-skinned but had a distinctive oriental appearance. Oftentimes we would take the children to the store and tell them beforehand to call us Mommy and Daddy. This always got the attention of those around us because my wife is full-blooded American Indian and I am of Swiss descent. It was funny to see the expressions on everyone's face. The truth of the matter is, we are all one in Christ, and He could not care less about the exterior. He looks on the heart. Our experience with John's family served to remind me that we are all children of God and He loved us so much that He gave His life for everyone.

The next day Sandi and I went to Waikiki Beach in search of employment. As we were walking down Ala Moana Boulevard, a young man by the name of Tom pulled up beside us in his van and told us to get in. Tom happened to be the accountant for the corporation that left us stranded in paradise. The abrupt folding of the company did not affect him because he had his own accounting business and a secure home. Tom was very surprised that we appeared to be taking our misfortune in stride. I explained to him the blessings that God just gave us, then I told him our testimony and how the Lord provides for those who are willing to serve and trust Him.

Then, to our amazement, Tom handed me about $1,000 in cash. He also told us to meet him at that same location every week and he would give us all the money we needed so we could eat in restaurants every day while we were in Hawaii.

For some inexplicable reason, I had doubts about receiving money from him. Thus, the next words that came out of my mouth surprised even me. I told him that I could not take his money because he did not know what it was like to have everything and then have nothing. The statement must have been from God because of Tom's response.

He said, "Allow me to share my story with you." Tom was from the Philippines and began his story telling us about the time when the Marcos Regime took over. He shared with us that at one time he was extremely wealthy. In fact, his house was so big that he had never even counted how many rooms it had. He had a dozen house cleaners and butlers and a fleet of limousines. He had also owned various banks and businesses and acquired great wealth. He had everything in a natural life that one could possibly want—until the Marcos Regime rose to power. He shared a somewhat familiar story about the day he went from having everything to having nothing.

The Marcos Regime tracked him down because Tom was one of the elite in the country as far as wealth was concerned. As if losing his great fortune were not enough, the regime put him in prison with the guarantee that he would die there. The reason they did not kill him right away was that they wanted him to give them the names of his relatives. When he refused to give them any information, his incredible ordeal began. The first week they broke his legs, the next week they broke his arms, and then they broke his ribs. He was, of course, in excruciating pain constantly. They finally placed him in a cell so small he could not move. They did not allow him to eat or go to the bathroom. The temperature was over 100 degrees and he sat for days on end in his own excrement with bugs crawling all over him.

At some point when Tom reached a place of utter hopelessness and was on the brink of giving up, to his amazement, the prison door swung open. His mother, a poor woman by his previous standards, had taken her entire net worth, about $10,000,000 and paid an informant to have Tom released. The person she bribed also smuggled Tom and his entire family over to the East coast of the United States. After their arrival, Tom's mother worked as a house cleaner so he could go to school and become an accountant. A short time later, Tom and his family were able to move to Hawaii.

Upon hearing this remarkable story, I felt a little embarrassed. I told him that I would gladly accept his kind offer of financial assistance. I felt that he, even more than I, truly knew what it was like to have everything (materially speaking) and then to have nothing.

Sandi and I marveled at how quickly God seemed to open a door for us. He had provided a place to live, food, money, and a car along with the wonderful opportunity to witness for Him. Although I knew that it was not God's purpose for us to live in Hawaii the rest of our life, I also knew without a doubt that He was in control and that He would soon reveal His true purpose for allowing us to be *lost in paradise*.

In fact, it was our deepest desire to leave Hawaii as soon as possible. Our stay in paradise, however, like so many other strange events in our life, proved to be an adventure in trusting God. The trying of our faith does indeed develop character. One very important lesson I have learned from all of these unbelievable events is that all things truly are possible with God. We must never underestimate God's ability to see us through. In this case, our trust in God enabled Him to bless us to the extent that our situation, which would certainly have destroyed anyone trusting in natural wealth, began to seem more like a vacation. Although the rain falls on both the good and the evil, the difference is in their respective perceptions of the rain.

Our Lord provided our needs at every turn, and as I reflect on that time, I recall many strange events that made me laugh during our brief stay in paradise. In particular, I remember walking by myself on Waikiki Beach early one morning—about 7:00 a.m. The weather was pleasant—a typical 80 degrees with a subtle breeze. The sun was shining and up towards the hills north of the beach a beautiful rainbow appeared. It rarely rained on Waikiki Beach. It seemed to be a true paradise, at least from a tourist's perspective. As usual, I was on my way to enjoy a buffet breakfast with all the trimmings when suddenly I saw what appeared to be a sea creature rising up out of the water. As the unidentifiable figure staggered closer, I realized that it was no sea creature at all but a homeless woman. Her hair looked like seaweed and her body was covered with mud and dirt. As she approached me, I said hello.

For no apparent reason, she started to yell at me and said, "Who do you think you are?"

I told her my name was Ray and that I was just being cordial as I wished her a blessed day.

She interrupted me and said, "You have a lot of nerve standing on my property." She announced that I was on Paradise Island and that ever since the war people had been intruding on her home. She was finally getting sick of it.

Naturally, I felt sad for her, because apparently she had been homeless since the war and dwelt in psychological torment all those years since it ended. For a moment, I reflected on that day when Sandi and I almost ended up homeless. Because I lacked wisdom at the time I tried to reason with her. As I did, she yelled even louder and started hacking at me with her arms. I saw two police officers in the distance and wondered if they would think I was abusing her and arrest me. Rather than risk it and have to try to explain myself, I started running until I was clear of the situation.

As I sat in the restaurant comfortably enjoying my food, I began to reflect on what had just happened. I felt a mix of sadness and guilt. I knew how close Sandi and I had come to being in that same sad circumstance. Therefore, I thanked the Lord for our many undeserved blessings.

After breakfast, I started walking down the beach to the Hilton Hawaiian Village Resort where Sandi worked. I stopped along the way and sat down on a park bench. The sun felt so good. I stretched out, laid my head back, and began taking in the warm, soothing rays. What bliss. Then I suddenly felt something hit me. I looked down and realized it was a pelican bomb. The damage was so vast that I had to throw away that shirt and buy a new one. When I met Sandi for lunch, I told her that the day was certainly not starting out too well.

I could only hope it would get better as I headed into work later that afternoon at the security company that had recently hired me. As I was on my way to the car after work that evening, two female prostitutes suddenly and inexplicably attacked me. Apparently, their business was a little slow that night, and they were trying to entice me into a bad situation. I managed to get away intact and proceeded to go pick Sandi up at work. "Dear," I said, "I am glad this day is finally ending."

With both of us working, we started saving a little money so that someday in the not-too-distant future we would be able to leave this tropical paradise.

A short time later, we received the unsettling news that Sandi's mother in New York was recovering from a heart attack. We knew that we would need approximately $2,000 to fly home as soon as possible. That night we earnestly prayed and believed that the Lord would meet our sudden need. Even though I knew I could ask Tom for the money, I felt that God would provide for our need. When we went to the post office to pick up our mail the next day, we were pleasantly surprised to find in one of our letters a check for exactly $2,000 from a couple in New England. The Lord had used us to help save this couple's marriage several years earlier. The Lord's timing is always perfect.

We said farewell and expressed our sincere gratitude to John and his family, as well as to Tom, and then anxiously boarded a plane destined for New York. As I reflected on all the answered prayers, I reminded Sandi that we have to be careful in what we ask of God.

As I looked back and tried to determine exactly why God allowed us to go to Hawaii, my thoughts returned to that Christmas when the company closed. Both our daughters were visiting us for the holidays, which was such a blessing. The only reason they were able to visit was that were able to obtain tickets several months earlier when things were going well. I remember opening the refrigerator that Christmas day and finding four hot dogs with no buns. Although the Christmas dinner itself wasn't too appealing, that evening the four of us went and sat on the beach together and praised God. At least we were together, healthy, and full of God's joy. Even then, we knew in our hearts that somehow God would work everything out.

The question persisted: *Why did all of this happen?* Then I recalled that moment when I received a call from the CEO of the company that left us stranded in paradise. One day after abolishing all of our resources, he had the nerve to ask me for a favor. I thought to myself, *Is God testing me? Would I be able to forgive this man and be the Christian example that the Lord desires?* I told him I would do him a favor on one condition. He agreed. My condition was that I share my testimony with him. I then told him about the love of Christ and the mighty things that God had done for Sandi and me throughout our lives. He listened quietly to what I had to say. Then he told me that he was in American Samoa and for some reason could not use the telephone system to call Canada. He gave me the telephone number of his mother who lived in Canada and asked me if I would call her and give her his number so that he could wish her a Merry Christmas.

I immediately called his mother. After I told her who I was and why I was calling, she began to weep. When I asked her what was wrong, she replied, "Praise God."

Taken aback, I said, "You're a Christian!"

"Oh, yes," she replied as she began to thank me. She shared with me that for the past seven years, she had fasted three days each month. In her prayers she had asked God to send someone into her son's life who would witness to him. She had not heard from her son for seven years until that day.

As I reclined in my seat on our flight to New York, it finally occurred to me. *Why could I not see it before?* I realized that the main reason God allowed us to be lost in paradise was to bless this faithful woman and answer her prayers. The fortunes of that company meant very little to God, but the people involved meant *everything* to Him. After all, He had no trouble meeting our every need without the bank accounts and resources of that company.

From our experience during this unique season in our life, I encourage others to open up their hearts and become available to listen to that still small voice of the Lord. What a joy it is to realize that God is concerned with our every need. Regardless of what the circumstances may look like, He is in control when we give Him control. From my experience of being lost in paradise, I can appreciate what the Apostle Paul said:

Philippians 4:11-13 says:

"Not that I speak in respect of want: for I have learned, in whatsoever state I am, therewith to be content. I know both how to be abased, and I know how to abound, everywhere and in all things I am instructed, both to be full and to be hungry, both to abound and to suffer need. I can do all things through Christ which strengtheneth me."

He will not only direct your path, He will supply your every need, in His time, for His purpose, and for His Glory. Indeed, we can be content in whatever circumstances we face, knowing that we can do all things through Him who strengthens us (Philippians 4:8, 11).

CHAPTER EIGHT

HIS AMAZING GRACE

THE LORD HAS a time and season for all things, that He may be glorified. After we arrived in New York, we went to the apartment building where Sandi's mother and sister lived. The apartment unit was too small for all of us, so we needed to look for another place to live. With His usual punctuality, God opened a door, and the next day we met a couple at church who invited us to live with them until we were able to get back on our feet. It was a beautiful home, secluded in the woods, up on a hill overlooking a lush valley. Our stay here proved to be an incredible two weeks of refreshing. During that week of relaxation, we were so thankful to the Lord for bringing us through.

One sunny afternoon, we decided to go to the grocery store to buy some food from the deli for a picnic. Soon after we ate, I started to feel sick to my stomach. My fever shot up to about 104 degrees, and I felt like I was going to die. Sandi took me to the hospital, where they diagnosed me with food poisoning. Although they wanted to keep me in the hospital, I refused and went back to the home where we were staying at the time. When we arrived, Sandi put her hands on my back and started to pray. Instantly, I could feel the poison in my system leave my body. It was beyond incredible.

After staying with this gracious couple for about two weeks, Sandi went to work at a beauty shop. That same day, she met one of the beauticians who was leaving the area. She told Sandi that she lived right down the street and asked if she was interested in a place to live rent-free. Oh, and we would also receive a small salary for taking care of an estate for an elderly couple. We came to a mutual agreement, and the Lord once again provided us with a place to live. It was so convenient because it was right down the street from where Sandi was working and only a mile from her mother's apartment. Praise God.

Blessed with a place to stay along with a small salary just to watch over an elderly couple, we had a lot of free time. At this point, Sandi and I had the opportunity to co-pastor a church on the Indian Reservation. The church received us with open hearts. Furthermore, God used us to extend the ministry by visiting many homes of Indians on the Reservation who did not go to church. During this period the Lord also opened a door for me to attend college for a half year, free of charge. In this experience, the Lord blessed and inspired me, helping me attain an A average in all subjects including accounting, business management, psychology, English, travel & tourism, and several other subjects.

The year 1993 would prove to be another trying year. Both Sandi's mother and a close friend had to go into a nursing home. We went to visit them every day for six months and eventually established a ministry at the nursing home. We were able to minister and witness to many elderly people.

Unfortunately, my wife's mother hated the nursing home. Her only friend was a man named Miles. Miles was a special man. Sandi and I had known him for several years. He was a Native American and up until the age of 72 had never been sick in his life. When he was young, his wife left him, and he raised ten children on his own. He never attended church because he did not want anything to do with what he perceived to be a "white man's religion." His perception, however, would soon change. In the last six months of his life, he had problems with his liver. Although he had never consumed liquor, his liver was failing, and his condition grew ever more serious. For six months, Sandi compassionately witnessed to Miles and was finally able to lead him to Christ. Indeed, I have never seen such a dramatic change in someone.

I remember the great sadness we felt when Miles died. One day we rushed him to the hospital as he was in great pain and in critical condition. As we were standing by his bedside, we witnessed his entire system shut down. As he lapsed into a coma, his eyes remained open as they dried up in their sockets.

Several hours elapsed as his body continued to shut down. About 10:30 p.m. that same day, as I began to pray, the Lord urged me within my spirit that Sandi desperately needed to pray with Miles. As she laid her hands on his head and started to pray, tears began flowing down her face. This man had become like a father to her. She loved him dearly. As she was praying, the Lord gave her a vision to comfort her. The room filled with clouds and she saw the sky open up. Then she noticed two large hands reaching out. At that moment, she asked the Lord if He would grant her a favor. She wanted to walk to Heaven's gate with Miles and escort him into the loving arms of Jesus. As she witnessed the two hands reaching out of the clouds, suddenly she saw Miles walking into those hands. Before he walked into the arms of Jesus, he turned around and smiled at her. At that precise moment he died. Although we had just lost a dear friend, we experienced a sense of great joy knowing that Miles was finally home.

Several months later, as we were visiting the nursing home one afternoon, Sandi's mother slipped into a coma. As we started to pray, her mother suddenly opened her eyes.

She said, "Sandi, this place is so beautiful. Oh, it is so beautiful," and then she closed her eyes and went to be with the Lord.

At the exact moment she died, her roommate was watching a movie on TV, and a song started to play. It was her mother's favorite song *Amazing Grace*. This brought Sandi great comfort because the Lord in His mercy was confirming that this day her mom was in Paradise.

After Sandi's mother died in the fall of 1993, we felt that our time and purpose in New York was complete. One day as we were reading the newspaper, we noticed the following advertisement: "Couple wanted to manage a resort in the Florida Keys." We submitted our résumé and a few days later received a phone call in reference to our applications. The woman on the other end reported that she had received about 75 applications, but for some reason she felt led to call us in for an interview. After a successful interview, in no time at all we were hired and on our way to the Florida Keys.

The weather there was beautiful indeed, and it appeared that we were once again in paradise. Not long after our arrival, I asked the Lord to confirm somehow that this was where He wanted us to be.

Our very first day, as I was walking around the premises, I decided to check out their beautiful swimming pool. I noticed that there were two people on opposite ends of the pool. I quickly sensed that something was definitely wrong. At one end of the pool, an elderly woman in her 90s was gasping for air, apparently drowning. At the other end of the pool was her daughter (who was the president of the association). The daughter was trying frantically to swim to her mother but could not reach her. I rushed over and dove into the pool. Thank God, I was able to save the older woman's life. This certainly was a confirmation from the Lord that I was in the right place at the right time. As usual, His timing is perfect.

We managed this property for a year and a half before we began to receive incredible persecution. A member of the condominium association board turned out to have a very hostile attitude toward Christians. On many occasions, she made up lies about Sandi and me and tried to sow discord wherever possible. After prayerful consideration, we left on our own. Although we did not know where we were to go, we knew however that it was time to leave the Keys.

We drove to Key Biscayne, Florida, which is just east of Miami Beach and stretches about six miles out into the water. We applied to manage a condominium on the island, and they hired us immediately. We managed that property for almost a year before once again receiving tremendous religious persecution. The enemy used a board member on that condominium association to antagonize us, and we knew that our season there was about to end.

We heard about an exclusive 120-unit condominium complex situated on the beach in Key Biscayne, so we went and applied. They hired us immediately, and it proved to be an incredible blessing. We received a blessed salary, along with a free, three-bedroom condominium and all utilities paid. God's timing in this matter was perfect, as usual, because our youngest daughter Patty had just moved down from New York to live with us.

As time went by, we began to feel a void in our life. Each night we would walk along the beach and pray, asking the Lord to make a change in our life. Although we now had material security, the desire of our heart was to work in ministry.

A short time later, the president of the association of condominiums we were managing found out that we were Christians. The persecution flared up once again, and a few months later, he made the decision not to renew our contract. Although we were sad, we also knew that the Lord was answering our prayers.

Before the persecution started, the Lord allowed a special blessing to take place. The couple who had blessed us with $2,000 when we were lost in Hawaiian paradise had unfortunately decided to get a divorce. Afterwards, the wife and her three children decided to move to West Palm Beach to be in Florida with her parents. Since this was only about an hour north of where we were living, we were able to go and visit them.

It was a sad situation. She did not have a car and she wanted to go to school and work to support her children. It was inconvenient to borrow her parents' car all the time, but under the circumstances, it was all she could do. At that time, we owned two cars. The Lord then spoke to us and told us to give both of our cars away. We quickly obeyed and gave one of our cars to someone who needed transportation. With the other car, we were able to bless one of our dear friends in need. Although the car was a blessing for our friend, it certainly did not lack its own dramatic history.

Two and a half years earlier, on a clear moonlit evening in Syracuse, New York, having just purchased that car we decided to take an evening drive around a new housing development. The street we turned onto was dark with hardly any streetlights. I stopped at the first home we came upon and proceeded to back into what I thought was part of the driveway. Suddenly, there was a loud noise beneath the car. It stopped and refused to budge forward or backward. Sandi slowly opened the passenger door to look out, and then her face turned pale as she spoke these frightening words, "Don't open your door."

When I asked why, she replied, "You won't believe this, but our car is precariously balanced on a hundred-foot cliff."

Sandi crawled out of the car very slowly and made her way around the ledge. As she left the car, it began to shift, rocking slowly back and forth. When she made it to my side of the car, she opened my door and I got out very carefully. Once safe, I observed the balancing act the car was engaged in, just inches from falling off the ledge. Looking at the car, I doubted even a tow truck could save it. Nevertheless, they sent two trucks out and were able to rescue the car with virtually no damage. God had used one large rock to preserve both our lives and our car.

After giving the two cars away, the next day, true to form, the Lord opened the door for us to purchase a brand-new car. When our daughter Patty arrived, she also needed a car. She got a job at the Fox TV network in Miami and was soon able to purchase a good used car.

The month of February 1997 arrived and our current job contract had ended. They gave us three weeks to vacate the property. During the previous year, we were able to purchase in cash approximately $25,000 worth of furniture. Since we did not have much money or time to move, I put an advertisement in the local paper to sell our furniture. The Lord knew ahead of time exactly what furniture we needed to sell. I was able to sell most of our furniture for the modest sum of $3,000, mainly because we needed the money right away. I sold everything except our bedroom and dining room furniture, and God once again moved us on to new challenges.

CHAPTER NINE

PATHWAY TO PEACE

Numbers 6:24-26 says:

"The Lord BLESSES thee, and keeps thee: The Lord make his face shines upon thee, and be gracious unto thee: The Lord lift up his countenance upon thee, and give thee peace."

A FEW MONTHS BEFORE we left Florida, the Lord performed another miracle. Sandi was in a lot of pain and made an appointment to see a doctor. Several years earlier, they had diagnosed her with a form of arthritis, and both her hip and back had sustained significant damage. When Sandi went back to the doctor, we were all amazed. After a complete examination, the doctor concluded that there was no arthritis remaining in her system at all. Praise God.

The day finally arrived for us to leave our condominium. We rented a storage area because like so many times before we had no idea where we were going or what we were going to do. Without too much worry, we stored the rest of our furniture and traveled around the state of Florida applying for various jobs. Later that same week we went to visit friends who lived north of Clearwater, Florida. We decided to stay with them for about a week while we were contemplating God's direction for our lives.

One day while staying at our friends' home I walked out on the back porch for a bit of fresh air. As I looked up at the beautiful clouds, my mouth dropped open in complete awe. Right before my eyes, I saw a figure with long hair and dressed in a long flowing robe appear and come forth from the clouds. With His arms outstretched, He began coming toward me. Then, as quickly as it had come, the vision was gone. Although I hesitate to attach any great theological significance to this appearance, I do believe that the Lord was lovingly assuring me that everything was going to work out fine.

By the beginning of April, as we had just finished celebrating my birthday, the Spirit of the Lord revealed to me that we were to move to Tulsa, Oklahoma. Since our daughter Patty had graduated from Oral Roberts University in 1993, we felt that she could easily get a job there. It was at this time that the Lord prompted me to write a book titled *Tell Him With Your Heart*. This revelation caused great excitement within my heart; this was something God had been preparing me to do for a long time. I firmly believe that God gives us the desires of our heart to fulfill His mighty plans for His glory.

Therefore, I encourage anyone reading this book to go for that dream that God has placed in your heart. Do not let the enemy, or anyone else for that matter, ever stop you from giving up that dream that God has entrusted to you. Although this book contains only a small glimpse of the many miracles the Lord has done in our lives, I am sure it will encourage and bless many, both financially and spiritually.

The night before we were going to move to Tulsa, I received a phone call from a woman who offered me a position as manager of an exclusive condominium complex located on the east coast of Florida. The package would include a condominium plus a very sizable salary with benefits. For some reason, I knew that if I accepted this incredibly generous offer

I would be accepting the security of this world again, rather than trusting in the Lord for the things that I could not yet see with my eyes. Thus, I refused the offer, and at that moment I made up my mind that I would follow the vision that I firmly believed was from our Lord.

We arrived in Tulsa, Oklahoma, on April 11, 1997, to begin our new life. As we started to unload our truck, we suddenly realized our furniture was too heavy to handle alone. I sent my daughter over to Oral Roberts University and told her to find a few strong men to help us move into our apartment. After some time, my daughter came back not with two men but with one young woman. When I thought about the load waiting for us in the truck, I reminded my daughter that I had asked her to go and get a few good *men*. Unfortunately, the young woman felt bad, so I invited her to come in. At that time, I felt led to pray for her. She told us that she had been sick. We prayed and the Lord healed her. I then thanked God, believing this was confirmation that Patty had found the right person for the job.

With our new friend's assistance, we were able to move 90% of our furniture into the apartment. I told the young woman helping us to see if she could find one strong man to help me with the rest of the furniture. She found someone walking by our apartment and was able to secure his help. The young woman helping us, whose name was Sandra, was about to graduate from Oral Roberts University and was trying to raise money to go on a mission trip to Africa. We were able to bless her with some money and quickly developed a close friendship with her. Sandra invited us to her graduation so that we could meet her family. It was a blessing to realize that God was confirming His Word through us.

We are confident that the Lord will use the *Tell Him With Your Heart* project and that it will ride the morning winds to the farthest oceans to glorify Him.

We know without a doubt that the enemy is truly powerless when faced with the power of one who has Christ living in him. If God is for us, then who can possibly be against us (Romans 8:31). He is always our help in time of need. We resided in Tulsa for 18 months until circumstances dictated that it was time to leave. Our daughter was fully established and happy to stay, but sad that we had to leave.

As we continued on our journey and walked down the pathway to peace, we knew in confidence that our Lord would guide and direct our every step. In October of 1998, Sandi and I accepted the inspiration of the Lord to move back to Florida with the confidence that our continued walk through life would bring a smile to the face of our Lord Jesus.

Just before we left Tulsa, we applied to an ad in the paper for a couple to manage a children's home in Florida. The ministry was on 40 acres of land with many homes to accommodate children. They had just completed a 14-bedroom home that we were to live in and take care of 12 children. We lived and worked there for six months. Many precious memories came out of this particular season that will forever be a blessed memory.

(Our five precious grandchildren)
We are all children of the living God

CHAPTER TEN

REFLECTIONS

A s I REFLECT on our journey thus far, there are so many more miracles and incredible memories yet to share. Here are just a few additional stories that I feel led to share.

I recall the day back in Hawaii when Tom, the former accountant in the property development corporation that closed suddenly, handed me a large amount of cash so that Sandi and I could eat at the finest restaurants. Tom told us that his elderly mother (in her 80s) had cancer and was not feeling well. Sandi and I asked if we could come over and pray for her. Although Tom was not a Christian, he trusted us and was willing to accept any possible help and hope for his mother. When we arrived at his house, Sandi sat down with Tom's mother. From the start, there was a language barrier because Tom's mother could only speak and understand her native language from the Philippines. We are well aware that with God there is no language barrier, so Sandi put her trust fully in Him.

Each woman began to speak in her own language, and somehow the Spirit allowed her to understand each other. After a pleasant visit and a special time of prayer, we left. Tom called us and told us that his mother was healed of cancer. God allows us to call on Him in faith, and if our request lines up with His timing and purpose, for His glory, nothing can stop His mighty hand and blessing!

In the early 1980s, we took our young teenage daughter who had just broken her arm to an evangelistic healing service a friend was hosting in southern New Hampshire. The Lord miraculously healed her broken arm in the cast!

Another miracle occurred in the late 1980s when we were visiting our daughter in Tulsa, Oklahoma. We had just picked up our luggage at the Tulsa airport and boarded the hotel service van to go to ORU when I noticed in the distance a large tornado that appeared to be at least a mile in diameter. As we drove to the hotel, the tornado seemed to follow us. There were moments when the effects of the twister was shaking our van with such force that it was hard to keep it on the road. When we reached the hotel outside of ORU, the tornado took a quick turn to the north and missed us by one street. There was extensive damage to both houses and cars. I believe wholeheartedly that the Lord had His hand of protection on us that day and steered the winds for our protection.

The Lord has blessed us in so many ways. On at least a dozen occasions, Sandi has experienced the visitation of angels.

On one occasion during the mid-1980s, Sandi went to the Boston Hospital for Women for a prenatal check-up. They had to abort her pregnancy due to complications that we never really understood. Apparently, during the procedure, Sandi died. Praise God, however, for the hand of the Lord brought her back and allowed me to continue my incredible journey with the love of my life. His grace and mercy is beyond amazing.

I am very careful when it comes to prophecy, especially when someone says, "I have a word from the Lord for you." On so many occasions, I have seen this gift abused. On one occasion, however, I recall how a word from the Lord truly amazed me. It came during a prophetic concert at a church in southern New Hampshire during the summer of 1990. I was serving as public relations director and concert promoter for the event. Sandi and I were reluctant to go, but the Lord seemed to be urging us to attend, so we went. On the way there I asked the Lord to show us somehow if this prophetic event were true.

I told the Lord (as if I could control His desire—silly me) to validate the prophecy in this way—if we were called upon to stand up and were prophesied over, we would hear the following words: "You have been waiting seven years for something, and it is about to be revealed." In this way, we would know that the message was from the Lord and bore His stamp of approval. When we arrived at the conference, we sat in the very back of the church. Approximately 1,500 people attended. The conference started and a speaker from Canada (whom we had never met) immediately asked Sandi and I to stand up. I could not believe it. I said to myself, "Okay, here we go, God; let us see what the man has to say to my reluctant spirit."

The man opened up with these words: "You have been waiting for something for seven years now and God will soon reveal it."

Well, obviously, I was in shock over his opening statement, but we attentively stood and listened. He then said, "Later this year, no one will know you." Not to boast, but I was rather popular because of my involvement in radio and concert promotion, and many people in New England knew who we were. As it turned out, shortly after that prophecy I received a phone call with that offer in Hawaii that would cause us not only to be lost in paradise but truly to go to a place where no one knew us. WOW! What can I say?

In the early part of 2006, I was managing a condominium complex near Miramar, Florida. We had been there several years (and once again, how we got there was another miracle), but the condominium was changing boards and that meant that I would probably lose my job. Sandi and I prayed and the Lord led me to call a particular Management Company to see if they had any openings anywhere in the state. They told me they had an opening in Orlando, Florida, and hired me on the spot to start in a few weeks. The salary was great with incredible benefits that included full insurance coverage for both of us. I accepted the position and we moved to Orlando.

The Lord impressed upon me that this tenure would last five years. After my second year, they gave us a very large three-bedroom condominium with a two-car garage to live in. We lived there five years. They ended up letting us go because Sandi and I had donated too much of our money to the Christmas party for the residents three months earlier. We then had two years off. Even though our two daughters are extremely financially secure, we hesitate to intrude too much on them with our burdens.

In October of 2012, it seemed like we were on our last leg again, but once again God came through and opened another door of management (perfect timing as usual). As I am writing this, we are into 2015 and still residing in Orlando, Florida, until the Lord opens up the next door for us to journey through. I must reiterate that during the past 49 years Sandi and I have been together we have moved an astonishing 70 times. (That's right, 70!)

In the spring of 2010, another incredible dilemma occurred when Sandi took a doctor's recommendation and underwent major back surgery. The surgery would involve extensive work on her lower back, which included a donor bone implant along with implanting at least 32 bolts and screws into her spine. So much took place during this trying time, but I will share some of the incredible highlights. Late that evening after the surgery, I left Sandi's bedside and went back home to get some rest so I could come back early the next morning. I went to sleep a little after midnight, and at the time I felt perfectly fine except for my deep concern for my wife and her well-being as I wondered if she would ever walk again.

I woke up an hour later with the most excruciating pain I ever had around my heart. Every breath I took felt like a knife penetrating my chest. In fact, I was struggling to survive with every breath I took. Although I should have called 911 immediately, I honestly felt that if I went to the hospital and my wife found out about it the news might kill her by causing intense grief in her fragile post-op state. So I prayed to God to heal me so that my wife would not have to know.

I struggled to stay alive and prayed because I was in intense pain for the next five-plus hours. When it seemed the Lord was not giving any positive response, I finally realized that God was not going to heal me at this moment in time and I had to get to the hospital right away. So I called my daughter in Long Island and told her what was happening and then made my way to the car and drove myself to the same hospital where my wife was.

When I arrived at the hospital, they immediately sent for a helicopter to transfer me to another hospital in downtown Orlando because of the seriousness of my condition and the fact that without urgent treatment I could die at any moment. At the destination hospital, they immediately took me into a surgical suite and called a heart specialist. They assigned me to one of the best heart surgeons available. He diagnosed me with congestive heart failure and said I very well could have died because my lungs were full of fluid. He treated me accordingly and assigned me to a private room for recovery. Both our daughters came to see me. One flew down from Long Island, New York, and the other flew down from Tulsa, Oklahoma. My wife still did not know anything about my situation as she continued recovering from her back surgery.

The evening before my daughters arrived at the hospital where my wife was staying, someone appeared to Sandi in a vision and comforted her, telling her not to worry about her husband because he was going to be just fine. When my daughters told Sandi what had actually happened, her first reaction was to obtain permission to leave the hospital for the day to go visit me. Although the doctor did not really want her to go, he allowed it because of her desperate appeal. When they released me after a week of treatment and medication, I was able to visit Sandi at the Celebration Hospital where she was staying.

The day finally came for Sandi's transfer to a rehabilitation facility. She had major problems at the facility (which I will not discuss at this time), so they moved her to another facility for recovery. She stayed at the new recovery facility for almost two months before they released her to come home. It was such a trying ordeal, but with God's grace, we made it through.

I thank the Lord that I had a great doctor. I also thank Him for sustaining me even through my stubbornness and allowing me to stay alive through that grueling six hours of agony. I thank Him for keeping my wife safe during her long, painful recovery.

I must add that a year later Sandi had to go into the hospital again and have the 32 bolts and pins removed from her spine because of the negative effect they had on her nerves. There is so much more to this story, but I just felt led to share some of the special moments when the Lord held our hands.

This is not Heaven, and we really do not deserve anything. Sure, according to the Scriptures, you can ask the Lord for anything believing and receive it, but the Word of God is clear. The reason He does anything is for His glory. He has a time and a purpose for all things. The truth is, while we were yet sinners He gave His life at Calvary for all and has prepared a place in eternity for us. We live in a world that has not changed much over the centuries; we still want what we want when we want it. We are here to serve and glorify our King. Know that His promises are true: If we acknowledge Jesus, accept Him, and ask for forgiveness, He will carry us to Paradise for eternity in a place of no more pain, tears, or sadness with the privilege of laying our crown at His feet.

Another incredible trial occurred during the summer of 2005 when Sandi's father passed away. A year and a half earlier we had gone to visit him before he first went into a nursing home. While we were there, he had a severe stroke and could not talk, walk, or even recognize who we were. God moved His mighty hand again. My precious wife put her loving hands on her dad, and as tears flowed in abundance from her beautiful eyes, she started to pray. Within the hour, her father could speak, comprehend, and walk. He knew who we were, and he was happy and thankful for such a loving daughter.

When the appointed time came for Sandi's father to enter the gates of Heaven, Sandi received that dreadful call from the nursing home that her dad had fallen onto his bedroom floor and died just after getting back from dinner at the nursing home's cafeteria. We called our daughters and their families and shared the bad news. They made arrangements and flew down to the west coast of Florida for the funeral. An elderly Mennonite nurse at the hospital sent Sandi a letter and told her that just before her father left the cafeteria that day and went back to his room where he fell and died, he mentioned to her that he had accepted the Lord in his heart based on the many years of ministering from his daughter. What a special confirmation and blessing to receive during a great time of sadness.

Soon after that, we left and drove back to Miramar, Florida, where we lived. My wife was feeling very sick and could not understand what was happening to her. She was on the verge of passing out, so I took her to the nearest hospital. They admitted her and performed extensive tests. The doctor came out and told me that he could not explain how Sandi was able to walk and function. He told me that her blood cells were so depleted it was if she was in the final stage of cancer, and she could die at any time. The first night in the hospital, they treated her with transfusions and special medication to try to bring her blood counts back to safe levels. They were unsuccessful, and her prospects of recovery looked bleak. I went into the room to pray with her, and she told me she had a vision. The Lord told her that she had a choice: She could either enter Paradise or return to her earthly life and continue on her journey with me. She chose to hold my hand for as many years as the Lord would allow, and within three days, all of her blood levels were normal. Once again, I was elated over God's mercy and grace.

There is another precious story hidden in the inner corners of my mind that brings tears to my being when I think about it. During the 1980s when I was managing, promoting, and working with many artists and bands, I knew a young man named Pete whose story I must share with you.

I first met Pete one evening during the fall of 1980 when Sandi and I walked into a restaurant with the intention of just having a good meal. To our surprise, a singing duo was performing for the guests' enjoyment.

We were amazed at Pete's incredible talent and gift for music. We became friends and from time to time, I would book him and his partner for various venues. As the years passed, our relationship and contact with Pete seemed to fade as dust in the wind. During December of 1988, a few weeks before Christmas, Sandi and I were shopping in a mall in Manchester, New Hampshire. As we were about to leave the mall, we passed a homeless person sitting on a bench. Something caused me to peer over at him, and to my surprise, it was Pete. I could barely recognize the incredible, talented artist with whom we had experienced so many fond memories. As I approached him and asked him how he was doing, I noticed that he was weak and seriously undernourished. When I asked him what he was doing these days, he hesitated to tell me anything and told me that he lived just a short walk from the mall.

I asked Sandi to stay at the mall and continue shopping while I went out for a short walk to Pete's home. As we left the warmth of the mall and entered what seemed to be some remote planet with the temperature hovering slightly above zero and blowing snow, Pete proceeded to lead me aimlessly through the blinding snow. We left the parking lot, crossed the main street, and drifted down some winding paths until we eventually crossed some railroad tracks. Through the wind and driving snow, we must have walked a good half mile until Pete led me down a 150-foot embankment. We then made a few turns in the confines of dense woods.

Finally, we came upon a small pup tent nestled between some trees and secured weakly by several ropes. I asked Pete what this place was, and he replied that it had been his new home for the past several months. He graciously opened the entry and asked me to come in. As we went in, my heart felt like it wanted to crumble. There was no room to stand up and barely enough room for the two of us. I noticed a few cans of food over in a corner on the frozen dirt floor. Pete told me that was his pantry. In another corner of the tent I noticed four or five two-inch candles, which he told me was his means of keeping warm on cold nights. After we chatted a while in the bitter cold, I asked Pete to come with me. We made our way back through the driving snow to the protective warmth of the mall. After I located Sandi and shared what had happened, we left the mall and proceeded to our home.

We took Pete in and told him that he was going to live with us until I could secure some reasonable accommodations for him. Each evening when I would check on our children, I noticed something odd as I passed by the room where Pete was sleeping. I noticed that he was sleeping on the floor instead of on the bed. Apparently, the many months he had spent sleeping on a dirt floor had made a deep impact on his psyche. I knew it would take some time for him to accept his rescue from the shadows of despair. He lived with us for approximately two weeks before I arranged for him to take residence in another environment that would be conducive to proper rehabilitation.

At the time, I was working full-time at a non-profit radio station as well as serving in several ministries. One ministry was Helping Hands. In this ministry, I was working with several key persons in the community to help the homeless. One such person was the mayor of Manchester, New Hampshire. They were able to purchase an abandoned building downtown and convert it to apartments. They would take in homeless persons and give them a place to stay rent-free while they were transitioning back into what we consider "normal" society. The ministry would then set them up with various programs and ministries to supply food and obtain clothing and basic items needed to survive as well as employment. Once they were working and could meet their basic needs, the ministry would charge them a nominal rent fee to encourage them to be more responsible so that they could more easily transition back into society on their own. They were supplied transportation to attend a local non-denominational church. After Sandi and I left the area and moved to Hawaii, I lost touch with Pete and never really knew what became of him. I trust and believe that he made a commitment to Christ.

Sandi and I have shared so many other experiences in which we have seen the hand of our Lord at work in ordinary and extraordinary ways that could easily fill another book or two. Our purpose in sharing these stories is not in any way to boast or receive any glory or praise for ourselves. Rather, our purpose is to share part of our story with a hurting world in which so many people are in need to emphasize the *fact* that God's great love is for all His children. What He has done in our lives He can do in anyone else's life. He can see you through whatever challenges you are facing, just as He has been faithful *always* to see us through our challenges. No one's story is really any greater than anyone else's story. We are all created in the image of Christ to dwell on this earth for but a brief moment in time, and the choices we make affect not only ourselves but those we meet. If you really love the Lord, tell Him with your heart because He gave His heart for everyone. We are all sinners covered by His grace, and He has prepared for us a perfect place to dwell with Him forever. May you reach out and touch the hem of His garment.

The precious shadow of my smile

CHAPTER ELEVEN

LIFE IN HIM

The Word of the Lord proclaims in Revelation 3:5:

"He that overcometh, the same shall be clothed in white raiment; and I will not blot out his name out of the book of life, but I will confess his name before my Father, and before his angels."

LOOK AT THE four letters in the words that represent *life* as just one example of the Lord's masterful plan. The letter *L* stands for *love*. John 3:16-17 says:

"For God so loved the world that he gave his only begotten Son, that whosoever believeth in him should not perish, but have everlasting life. For God sent not his Son into the world to condemn the world, but that the world through him might be saved."

Love is certainly the most important attribute in life. It is truly representative of what God is, for "God is love" (1 John 4:8).

Mark 12:28-34 says:

"And one of the scribes came, and having heard them reasoning together, and perceiving that he had answered them well, asked

him, which is the first commandment of all? And Jesus answered him, the first of all the commandments is, Hear, O Israel; The Lord our God is one Lord: And thou shalt love the Lord thy God with all thy heart, and with all thy soul, and with thy entire mind, and with all thy strength: this is the first commandment. And the second is like, namely this, Thou shalt love thy neighbour as thyself. There is none other commandment greater than these. And the scribe said unto him, Well, Master, thou hast said the truth: for there is one God; and there is none other but He, And to love him with all the heart, and with all the understanding, and with all the soul, and with all the strength, and to love his neighbour as himself, is more than all whole burnt offerings and sacrifices. And when Jesus saw that he answered discreetly, he said unto him, thou art not far from the kingdom of God. No man after that asked him any question."

There were no more questions after that.

Matthew 5:43-48 says:

"Ye have heard said; thou shalt love thy neighbor, and hate thine enemy. But I say unto you, Love your enemies, bless them that curse you, do good to them that hate you, and pray for them which despitefully use you, and persecute you; That ye may be the children of your Father which is in heaven: for He makes his sun to rise on the evil and on the good, and sends rain on the just and on the unjust. If ye love them that love you, what is your reward? If ye salute your brethren only, what do you have more than others? That is what the publicans do. Be ye therefore perfect, even as God, which is in heaven perfect."

The letter *I* in **life** is **invitation**.

John 6:37-38 says:

"All that the Father giveth me shall come to me, and him that cometh to me I will in no wise cast out. For I came down from heaven, not to do mine own will, but the will of him that sent me."

Luke 15:10 says:

"Likewise, I say unto you, there is joy in the presence of the angels of God over one sinner that repenteth."

Can you believe that? We actually take part in the joy that takes place in the presence of the angels of God. It is certainly clear and to the point, especially in John chapter 1 where we see that there are even times when we are not welcomed among our own.

John 1:11-14 it says:

"He came unto his own, and his own received him not. But as many as received him, to them He gave power to become the sons of God, even to them that believe on his name: Were born, not of blood, nor of the will of the flesh, nor of the will of man, but of God, And the Word was made flesh, and dwelt among us, (and we beheld his glory, the glory as of the only begotten of the Father,) full of grace and truth."

Acts 2:21 says:

"And it shall come to pass, that whosoever shall call on the name of the Lord shall be saved."

Have you invited anyone today to come to the throne of God? God has made it clear that we should go into the entire world and preach the Good News. We are to be the invitation extended to those who do not know Christ, as Christ has invited and draws us unto Himself.

The *F* in *life* would appropriately stand for forgiveness.

Isaiah 1:18 says:

"Come now, and let us reason together, saith the Lord: though your sins be as scarlet, they shall be as white as snow; though they be red like crimson, they shall be as wool."

In 1 John 1:9, the Word proclaims:

"If we confess our sins, he is faithful and just to forgive us our sins, and to cleanse us from all unrighteousness."

When God forgets and forgives, there is no question about it.
Psalm 103:12 says:

"As far as the east is from the west, He removes our transgressions."

Certainly, we have a responsibility as lights that shine the love of Christ to demonstrate that kind of forgiveness in our own lives.
Mathew 6:14-15 says,

"For if ye forgive men their trespasses, you're heavenly Father will also forgive you: But if ye forgive not men their trespasses, neither will your Father forgive your trespasses."

The Lord Jesus is our perfect example.
Ephesians 4:29-32 warns:

"Let no corrupt communication proceed out of your mouth, but that, which is good to the use of edifying, that it may minister grace unto the hearers. And grieve not the Holy Spirit of God, whereby ye are sealed unto the day of redemption. Let all bitterness, and wrath, and anger, and clamour, and evil speaking, be put away from you, with all malice: And be ye kind one to another, tenderhearted, forgiving one another, even as God for Christ's sake hath forgiven you."

The *E* in *life* represents eternity. When we are aware that God has prepared a place for us, we look forward to the day when we will be in the Lord's presence forever.
1 Corinthians 15:51-58 declares:

"Behold, I shew you a mystery; we shall not all sleep, but we shall all be changed, In a moment, in the twinkling of an eye, at the last trump: for the trumpet shall sound, and the dead shall be raised incorruptible, and we shall be changed. This corruptible must put

on incorruption, and this mortal must put on immortality. When this corruptible shall have put on incorruption, and this mortal shall have put on immortality, then, it shall come to pass the saying; Death is swallowed up in victory. O death, where is thy sting? O grave, where is thy victory? The sting of death is sin; and the strength of sin is the law. Thanks to God, He gives us the victory through our Lord Jesus Christ. Therefore, my beloved brethren, be ye steadfast, unmovable, always abounding in the work of the Lord, forasmuch as ye know that your labor is not in vain in the Lord."

Of course, eternal life is possible because Christ Jesus gave His whole self and heart for all of us. It is important to remember that while we were yet sinners, before we were even born, God knew the day would come that we would submit to Him. He knew that the only way that we could be justified was for God Himself to come to earth in the form of a man and give His life and take upon Himself the sins of the world He did this so that through Him *we* might be saved and *He* might be glorified.

John 11:25-26 declares:

"Jesus said unto her, I am the resurrection, and the life: he that believeth in me, though he was dead, yet shall he live: And whosoever liveth and believeth in me shall never die."

Our God is a just and good God.

Romans 6:22-23 says:

"But now being made free from sin, and become servants to God, ye have your fruit unto holiness, and the end everlasting life. For the wages of sin is death; but the gift of God is eternal life through Jesus Christ our Lord."

Finally, think on these things that God has proclaimed!

In Philippians 2:1-11, we read these eloquent words inspired by the Lord Himself:

"If there be therefore any consolation in Christ, if any comfort of love, if any fellowship of the Spirit, if any bowels and mercies, Fulfil ye my joy, that ye be likeminded, having the same love, being of one accord, of one mind. Let nothing be done through strife or vainglory; but in lowliness of mind, let each esteem others better than themselves. Look not every man on his own things, but every man also on the things of others. Let this mind be in you, which was also in Christ Jesus: Who, being in the form of God, thought it not robbery to be equal with God: But made Himself of no reputation, and took upon him the form of a servant, and was made in the likeness of men: And being found in fashion as a man, he humbled himself, and became obedient unto death, even the death of the cross. Wherefore God also hath highly exalted him, and given him a name which is above every name: That at the name of Jesus every knee should bow, of things in heaven, and things in earth, and things under the earth; And that every tongue should confess that Jesus Christ is Lord, to the glory of God the Father."

The Holy Spirit will guide me in all truth

CHAPTER TWELVE

A WORD FROM THE AUTHOR

I T IS COMMON knowledge that there are several facts one must know and accept to become a Christian. First, you must acknowledge that Jesus Christ died for your sins. The Word of God says in Acts 2:21:

"It shall come to pass, that whosoever shall call on the name of the Lord shall be saved."

John 6:38:

"For I came down from heaven not to do mine own will, but the will of Him that sent me."

John 3:16:

"For God so loved the world that He gave His only begotten Son, that whosoever believeth on Him should not perish, but have everlasting life."

You must accept Christ into your heart:

John 14:6:

"Jesus said unto him, I am the way, the truth, and the life: no man cometh unto the Father, but by me."

John 6:37:

"All that the Father giveth me shall come to me; and him that cometh to me I will in no wise cast out."

Mark 12:30:

"And thou shalt love the Lord thy God with all thy heart, and with all thy soul, and with all thy mind, and with all thy strength: this is the first commandment."

You must ask forgiveness for your sins. The Word of God says the following:

Psalm 86:5:

"For thou, Lord, art good, and ready to forgive; and plenteous in mercy unto all them that call upon thee."

Psalm 103:12:

"As far as the east is from the west so far has He removed our transgressions from us."

Proverbs 28:13:

"He that covers his sins shall not prosper: but whoso confesses shall have mercy."

You must also be willing to obey His commandments:

Romans 2:6-8:

"Who will render to every man according to his deeds: To them who by patient continuance in well doing seek for glory and honour and immortality, eternal life: But unto them that are contentious, and do not obey the truth, but obey unrighteousness, indignation, and wrath."

1 Samuel 15:22:

"And Samuel said, Hath the LORD as great delight in burnt offerings and sacrifices, as in obeying the voice of the LORD? Behold, to obey is better than sacrifice, and to hearken than the fat of rams."

1 John 2:4:

"He that saith, I know him, and keepeth not his commandments, is a liar, and the truth is not in him."

The Word of God also says that we are to be separate from the world. 2 Corinthians 6:16-17:

"And what agreement hath the temple of God with idols? For ye are the temple of the living God; as God hath said, I will dwell in them, and walk in them; and I will be their God, and they shall be my people. Wherefore, come out from among them, and be ye separate, saith the Lord, and touch not the unclean thing; and I will receive you."

Remember that Romans 10:9 declares that when we confess with our mouth the Lord Jesus and believe in our heart that God raised Him from the dead, we shall be saved. We must also obey His Word and be separate from the world—not to be saved but to glorify God and enjoy abundant life in Him.

Have you noticed how both businesses and individuals respond to various situations and circumstances in the world around us? Unfortunately, attitudes and priorities depend on what you have, who you know, what you might inherit, or what you are worth in a tangible way.

How many people do you know who applaud royalty, athletes, movie stars, artists, singers, writers, and those who have attained great wealth either by their own works or by inheritance? How many times have you observed those in business or positions of influence show partiality or give favor to friends of the family or someone who knows someone?

Remember that we are all equal in God's eyes—whether it be a well-known evangelist or preacher, a large ministry, some other figure in a position to be idolized because he holds a position of status and influence, or one who may have attained great wealth or been blessed with great anointed gifts from the Lord. When you see people "idolize" such people, recall that the Lord says we are to be separate from the world.

I tell you this so that you will not be discouraged when you come to the realization that we have all come short of the glory of God. Forgive others as God has forgiven you. When you see Christians demonstrating attitudes similar to those who do not know Christ, you may feel the sadness that Christ feels.

Hebrews 12:2 says:

"Looking unto Jesus the author and finisher of our faith; who for the joy that was set before him endured the cross, despising the shame, and is set down at the right hand of the throne of God."

If the Lord was willing to give His life knowing that all would sin, then He already took into consideration the weakness of man.

John 8:7 says:

"So when they continued asking him, he lifted up himself, and said unto them, He that is without sin among you, let him first cast a stone at her."

I challenge you to be separate from the world and refuse to compromise in all areas of your life, even in ministry. You must be willing to lose everything you have knowing that Christ will supply your every need (Philippians 4:19).

Finally, yet importantly, do not be discouraged if someone tells you that the reason you are going through trials or are sick is that you either have sin in your life or are lacking in faith. Although this may be true in many cases, be comforted in the fact that there are exceptions and circumstances, which may be beyond our comprehension. Remember, God can turn *any* situation around.

Let us pray.

"Lord, we are to trust You with all our heart, mind, and soul. I know in confidence that You will direct my path. I thank You, Lord, for directing my path, and I ask that You direct the paths of

all who hear or read these words. My dear Lord, I love You more than words can say or express. I love You more than all the praises that have ever been shouted, or whispered. I worship You, Lord. I bow on my knees to You. I tell You with all my heart, I love You. I will do the things that You want me to do. I will always give thanks to You, Lord, and I believe whatever I ask I will receive, for Your glorification. I am well aware, Lord, that You have examined my heart and know all there is to know about me. When I cry tears of joy, I pray that all the angels of Heaven will praise You as they join with me in adoration of You, Father. I know You will make my path straight and give me rest among the still waters, as I need refreshing. I live in complete confidence that even if I were to ride the morning winds to the farthest oceans, even there I know that Your precious hand would guide me. For those times when I am in the shadows of this world, I know that I can rest assured that You will be the light around me. I thank you, my Lord, even for the valleys. Without them, I would not have seen the mountaintops. Forgive me, Lord. Forgive my sins as I forgive others. I recognize that You gave your life for me. Lord, may I continue to walk through life according to Your will, and may my life bring a smile upon Your face and cause the holy angels of Heaven to rejoice forever. Lord, when Your children look at my life may they see only You, and I pray that they also might say to the world, if you really love the Lord, tell Him with your heart. Your word is a lamp to my feet and a light to my path, and a love that burns within me. My heart is holding hands with You. Amen."

Blessings!

Made in the Master's image

CHAPTER THIRTEEN

INSPIRED POETRY

THE LORD HAS given me one of the desires of my heart—the desire to share my inspiration from Him. This inspiration is not only to receive but also to be able to interpret in the form of words and melodies from my heart so that others can be blessed and inspired. This chapter contains only a few of the many inspired moments the Lord has given me.

A Day in Your Field

Father, I thank You for accepting me as Your child. As a youth, I remember running in Your fields, surrounded by your eloquent beauty, delicately painted upon each flower. I felt as free as the morning winds and as secure as the birds that fill Your endless sky; then I paused and wondered why not everyone can see clearly. Occasionally, I would stop to lie down in one of Your soft meadows and then humbly allow the overwhelming comfort of your delicate nature to caress my back; it seemed to hypnotize my frail limp body. As I gazed upwards towards Your endless sky, I vividly remember having intimate thoughts of You, my dear Lord. I sometimes wondered what You really look like. Are there castles in Heaven? Can we fly there? How long will it be before I actually go there? What will I be doing when I get there? What is perfect peace really like? These and hundreds of other questions seemed to embrace my curiosity with an unending assault. At times, I would just lie in your fields in complete awe, with an innate appreciation of Your marvelous handiwork.

I loved to observe the puffy cumulus clouds, as they appeared as cotton candy, formed into glorious shapes by an unseen hand. As they pranced across Your endless ocean blue sky, I visualized the formations of what appeared to be animals, angels, people, cities, and palaces; and I embraced the thought, how satisfying it is just to dream. I began to realize that life itself was a state of constant change, and yet the echoing thought of words I heard in the past seemed etched in the far depths of my mind. You deliberately and compassionately placed them there by Your timely yet purposeful inspiration, and suddenly it appeared as though they dropped out of a perfect mold, which read so distinctly clear: One day all things will pass away, but Your love will last forever.

Dear Father, I thank You for the precious memories and the countless days spent going through the many fields of life. I hold on dearly to Your promise that it has not yet appeared what we shall be, but one thing is certain—one day we shall be like You. I thank You for assuring me that no one can separate me from Your love. As You continue to hold my heart in Your majestic hands, I will sing, "Holy are You, Lord," as I dwell in Your fields of Grace and Mercy forever.

I Pray Lord Jesus

I commit to You my Spirit, Lord
    Into Your hands receive,
    All the blessings You have bestowed on me
    Helping others to believe,

Through the laughter and the tears, life's trials,
    My faith, Your planted seed,
    All the joy the angels looked upon
    When salvation met my need,

I submit to You my eyes, my ears,
    Your Word directs my path,
    To feed the hungry, lost, those who thirst
    By Your mercy spared from wrath,

Sinful nature in a world so dark
    Your guidance is their light,
    Savior, Master, Holy Lamb of God
    Your forgiveness brings us sight,

I pray Lord Jesus
    May a double portion of Thy Spirit
    Fall on me,

I pray Lord Jesus
    Use me mighty in these last days that the
    World may see,

I pray Lord Jesus,
    I pray Lord Jesus through me

He Paid Full Price

When I began to realize that
Christ was who He said He was
The veil of earthly pride began to fade

To think, like men I was secure
In what I could hold
Within my hands

Moreover, that it would satisfy my very soul
In addition, win the prize, rise up applause
And seemingly at times, like a child
So immature, so young
I offered up such ugly motives
Out of touch
Just growing old
Allowing thorns to appear
As though sometimes unseen

I was fooling myself
For not controlling my own tongue
For if I took the time to look within myself
Not hide; surely, I would have shed the scales of time
That hid the only truth

In addition, at times, make believe, even say hello
Alternatively, openly give to those in need

That was only surface, self-centered lust
Just attributes of pride

For some people spend an entire lifetime
Searching and hoping to find
A pot of gold at the end of every rainbow

They accomplish any goal
> *They think that they have arrived on tangible ground*
> *That will give them peace of mind*

I tell you the truth, as I express how I feel
> *Do not look at life as though you have perfect vision*
> *For within each heart, there has been placed a special*
> *Part of the knowledge of God*

A closing thought, which goes beyond
> *Even a meaningful sacrifice, saved by grace*
> *Not any works that you are able to do or even take*
> *Credit for, and do not let the clock consume*
> *Those moments you could have spent with Him*
> *Not only is Christ the Lord and King*
> *Nevertheless, He came and paid full price*

God Is Everywhere to See

Oftentimes we look upon
The way we sometimes feel

In addition, question if there is a God
And if He is, how real

The evidence surrounds us all
And if you choose like me

The living God is everywhere to see
He made the stars, to light the night

As it that shines upon the manger
He lit the sun that shines with radiance

So bright, it softens anger
He brings a smile that embraces every face

When love fills up their heart
It is clear to me, the living God is everywhere to see

If you seek Him with your heart
You will find Him

If you call upon His name
You will surely hear love's sound

As angels sing and glory brings
The living God is everywhere to see

I Will Not Follow the Wind

I will not follow the wind
    Moreover, I will no longer sin

Now that my life has become
    More like You

I cannot quite walk on water
    But my heart
    Is changed

This very season
    Of my life
    Is made
    Brand new

Seasons change
    But your love
    Remains the same

There is a time and a place
    You know the day

Life remains a mystery for some
    However, for those you have called by name
    They shall hear your voice

Special Hands

Once there was a time
 When I saw dimly through life's haze

Now it is perfectly clear
 Your love deserves my praise

And if only for a moment's smile
 I bring upon Your face

You are that special hand that has held me up
 During those times, I lost my place

Now I know
 You are my Lord, my life
 Moreover, everything I do

There is a reason and a purpose
 Cause my life I live for You

Special hands that mold me
 Special hands that hold me
 Special hands that surely say
 I will carry you beyond life's shaded door

Or cruise on the waters be blessed and enjoy
 Discover a room with a view unsurpassed
 Then enjoy the finest in food, first class

Let the warmth and the wind caress me with care
 As nature unfolds all its glory to share

The lake reflects harmony like crystal it gleams
 Administering love aboard the ark of things unseen

A picture perfect melody, a caring time for all
 Awaits all who need quiet moments, reflections of God's call

If you just believe with your heart, His Word is true
     He will fulfill your vision make all things brand new

As an example to others that they might receive
     You need just to hold on, praise God, and believe

For Those Who Wait

When the sky forms one last rainbow
*   And there are no more leaves to fall*

Just take a closer look around you
*   There is still love if only you would call*

Upon the Lord in Heaven, upon the Lord so great
*   Upon the Lord, upon the Lord for those who wait*

When the clouds no longer paint the sky
*   And the grass is no longer green*

Just take a closer look around you
*   There is still love if only you would call*

Upon the Lord in Paradise, and His sacrifice
*   Upon the Lord, upon the Lord for those who wait*

We have fallen short of His glory
*   However, He came forgiving all our sins*

All pride becomes a faint dim shadow
*   For there's still love if only you would call*

Upon the Lord in Heaven, upon the Lord so great
*   Upon the Lord, upon the Lord for those who wait*

Upon the Lord in Paradise, and His sacrifice
*   Upon the Lord, upon the Lord for those who wait*

Holding Hands

You are the love of my life
  My dear precious wife

If I had only known
  That your heart was so true

I would have searched the world for you
  You are my dream that came true

Moreover, all that you do
  From your smile to your sweet caress

Taking a ride on the clouds
  Or holding you proud

Heaven has been so gracious because I am so blessed
  You were the gift when I prayed

Lord, bless me this day
  Lord, send me an angel to love

In addition, when I received
  That pure gift from above

Could hardly wait to say "I do"
  Now we both serve You as one

The true risen Son
  Comforting words to help us through

You have supplied all our needs
  And pruned all our weeds

We are so grateful for giving us You
  Even when the sun does not shine anymore

We will still be holding hands
  When we walk through that gate evermore

The Master will hold open the door
  Moreover, we will ride starlight

Gazing at eternity
And forever, my darling, my dear
We will be holding hands

Holy word that's true (Rapture song)

There is a host of angels
　　Soon coming in the clouds

And we as believers
　　Will be joining in this glorious crowd

The One who goes before us
　　Upon a white horse as flaming fire

With the sword of the Spirit
　　Holy Word that is true

Will change both Heaven and Earth
　　In addition, make it brand new

Then all of us together
　　With gather at the throne of God

Worshipping, praising, lifting holy hands
　　And proclaiming

The Lord is the Lord of all
　　The Holy King of Kings

Creator of all there is and more
　　That is why we sing

Holy, Holy, Holy is our Lord

Holy, Holy, Holy is our Lord

Holy, Holy, Holy is our Lord

Worshipping Him

When my Lord comes to take me home
>> *I will be willing to take His hand*

Take my life, Lord, and be glorified
>> *Let my crowns lay at your feet, my Lord, Amen*

I will ride the morning winds, my Lord, to Heaven
>> *I will walk on streets of gold, my Lord, and bow down*
>> *Worshipping, worship Him*

When my race is complete, fulfilled
>> *I will see glory beyond I will stand*
>> *Praising God for eternity*

We will sing worthy is our King
>> *We will ride the morning winds, dear Lord, to Heaven*
>> *We will walk on streets of gold, bow down to God*
>> *Worshipping*

Worship Him

Lord, I Love You

If I were to walk on water, Lord
    On the other hand, move each mountain away

Control the stars and have them shine
    To light my path each day

Direct the rolling seas to calm
    Make each rainbow born to stay

I would still be as a tinkling cymbal
    Or a clamoring sound with a need to pray

For You, O Lord, are mighty
    Your greatness beyond compare

And upon my works whether vast or great
    Your love I need to share

For when the sky is opened
    Moreover, Your appearing is in sight

To see Your smile with arms outstretched
    Bring such joy and surround me with Your light

But, Lord, before my time to go
    There is just one thing that the world must know

The way I feel inside
    I just cannot hide it anymore:
    Lord, I love you

More Than a Vision

There is a vision I have come to know
        Since sown by God can only grow

It has woven its way into my heart
        That is why I feel a special part

Of me, of you, and all of us who
        Are wrapped within a dream come true

I love my Lord in such a way
        It is hard to thank Him when I pray

I tell you this with love, press on
        Together we will complete His song

A rhapsody of destiny
        In perfect pitch, just watch and see

More than a vision, it is all that is true
        For the light of God is shining through

Do all you can and then just stand
        Then behold the Lord's miraculous hand

It is not as if God has not seen this before
        Though it seems that way, when the tide's at your door

His perfect peace is all you need
        Beware of the tempting trinket's seed

What could have been or might be if
        Does not compare with our Lord

It is more than a vision, you cannot explain
        If it is of God, His love will remain

God embrace you
        Squeeze out confusion in every way

Love, surround you with delight
        In addition, bring many smiles within His light,

All things someday will surely end
    Nevertheless, in between, we must let blend,
    Our hearts with Christ, always to lend

A listening ear to His still small voice
    His truth in wisdom the only choice

It is more than a vision a cherished dream
    The Lord's anointing upon the scene

A panoramic view of love
    Comes from the Lord of lords above

If He be for us then who against
    Do not sit with those upon life's fence

Walk beyond what you can see
    Then He will shape what you should be

In His image in the twinkling of an eye
    For He knows your purpose here and why

Take comfort in the great I Am
    He knew you while He formed you,
    Therefore, it is obvious that He knows all wrong

Let not your heart be troubled, no fear
    Moreover, in all you do, His way shall be clear

Within your heart is the Spirit's key
    That will unlock the door, to help you see

As the Lord fulfills your vision
    The time is close
    To be revealed in His season

Your purpose for living
    And knowing the reason

So look up, my child, and take His hand without
    Question

For faith is not what it seems
    But is learned in the lesson

I pray for your happiness
    Your joy I do share

Remember the One you can count on
    Is standing right there

Let His presence surround you
    Embrace you with mercy

No need to lack favor
    He knows when you are thirsty

Yes, today is a turning point
    So hold fast to your dream

He loves you and plans
    To keep you on His team

As It Was

As it was in the days of Noah
    Therefore, it shall be in the times near the end

Some will love their neighbor
    Others would crucify a friend

Times in which great knowledge will bring blindness
    Even love of self will betray the choice of right
    As it was, so shall it be, dark as the night

However, if you look within the distance
    There is a rainbow
    With all protection, care, and mercy for your walk

And if you take the time to ask God for His wisdom
    He will hold you safely, everlasting in His ark

For as it was in the days of Noah
    Love within your heart can bring His holy dove

Nevertheless, many shall forsake His words
    And others chosen, shall be embraced within His love

As it is and as it shall be, He alone has the plans
    No one can change the times or the seasons

Like those days gone by, they laughed at Noah
    It shall be just as it was

Tell Him with Your Heart

If you really love the Lord
    Tell Him with your heart

Do the things you know
    He wants you to do

Cause He loves you
    Cause He loves you
    Love Him, too

When living in the truth
    He becomes the greatest part of you

Give Him thanks for all the things He has done for you
    Cause He loves you
    Cause He loves you
    Love Him, too

In addition, whatever you ask in His name
    That will He do, that the Father

May be glorified
    May be glorified
    May be glorified
    In the Son

If you really love the Lord

Tell Him with your heart

Tell Him with your heart

Tell Him with your heart

I Am Glad

If I could stand on the top
  Of a perfectly formed rainbow

In addition, the Lord was so pleased
  He pulled back life's curtain, so

I could travel the rays
  Of a marvelous sunset

See the tops of each mountain
  Observe all His love, and all grace not forget,

Then I could hear the whispers of nature
  Moreover, sense all feelings in rhyme,

See how His hands formed the heavens
  In addition, hear the angels sing sometime

Then I could truly walk in His footsteps
  Life's veil lifted

In addition, more than that, who He is, and that He
  Chose to come and give His life, for everyone

The Message

There is a message in the wind
 Passing by this very day

It carries truth that has always been here
 Since He molded man, in His own way,

He placed the stars to light the darkness
 Sent the waters, formed the moon

Created man in His own image
 Then gave His life one afternoon,

He loved us long before we hurt Him
 Knowing sin would rule our life

But by His mercy and compassion
 He sent His Son, we know as Christ

You will find forgiveness in His presence
 For the asking, all you need

A healing touch of deep compassion
 All life is from His planted seed,

There is a message in the knowledge
 He has allowed you to obtain

So look within your heart to please Him
 Do all, in His name

One Day

One day as I observed the sky
  With all its beauty, I wondered why

Oftentimes with anguish pains
  It seems to weep, begin to cry

At times the tears came in abundance
  Even with great floods, sometimes they cover

Vast fields with flowers and sparkling valleys
  Try families' dreams, to find each other

Without notice, the sun appears in all its glory
  With splendor and radiance, to caress the earth

Embracing with its warmth, life's soothing cloak
  Rays reaching out, once again giving birth

Except a grain of wheat, falls fertile
  Beneath the stumbling feet of mortal man

There can never be new growth, new branches
  Without God's pruning, to fulfill His plan

Hold on to proclamations made
  Within the Word of God, it is sure

For He alone, brings all together
  To blossom in season, prompt change, make pure

One day, you too will notice nature
  With all its decay, it somehow holds on

We were once as a child, simply just not knowing
  The true reasons why, but for His glory we were born

One day you will speak His words with boldness
  Moreover, help change lives in Jesus' name

One day all tongues will confess our Savior
  In addition, shine for Him, which is why He came

Victory

Victory is born in the shout
    To our King, He is what we are about

To glorify Him, release our sin
    Thus the words, ye must be born again

Victory is through the name
    In the blood of the Lamb that was slain,

Who by His words, calmed the sea
    Healed the sick, saved the lost, you and me

Victory in nature and all life
    Consuming all of the causes of strife

Changing worry and grief into peace
    Since the star that appeared in the east

Victory holds on to the dream
    That, faith is but evidence unseen

If He be for us, then who against
    The choice is yours, stay off the fence

Father Forgive Them

Father, forgive them now

Father, they know not what
> *They have done*

I am their sacrifice
> *Lamb of God*
> *Slain for all*
> *Taking their shame*

Into Your precious hands
> *I commit to You*

Now our Spirits have become one
> *I am the risen Son*

Father
> *Father, forgive them now*

Father, they know not what
> *They have done*

Now they shall rise
> *Up on wings*
> *As eagles and fly*
> *They shall*

And they that choose life
> *Praise My Holy Name*
> *They shall*

I tasted death for everyone
> *Moreover, by My Grace, I welcome you*

Father, forgive them now

A Love Beyond Our Love

There is a love that goes beyond our love
  Changing lives and mending hearts, His love

Merciful, surrounding us with Grace
  There is a love
  There is a love

There is a love that goes beyond our love
  There is a love that goes beyond our love

Healing all diseases known, His love
  Fill me, Lord, by faith in You I live

There is a love,
  There is a love,

There is a love that goes beyond our love
  Transgressions far removed from every side
  Come quickly, Lord, we are your spotless bride

There is a love that goes beyond our love
  Pierced in His side, blood, does not lie, His love

Merciful, surrounding us with Grace
  There is a love
  There is a love

There is a love that goes beyond our love
  There is a love that goes beyond our love

Our Walk

We all must walk a path
*   And a Holy love to share with talk*

A winding road that weaves through life
*   Will surely try your heart with strife*

Nevertheless, hold on to His unseen hand
*   Will guarantee rewards that stand*

Far beyond any joy you may conceive
*   Is yours in time if you believe*

To live is Christ and death is gain
*   To share His Word will bless His name*

Give gifts to the needy, a deed that's lasting
*   Displaying the image of Christ, full of compassion*

For when our walk takes its last turn
*   Know the Kingdom of God is not simply earned*

Remember, it is grace alone that brings you home
*   All that lives the Word shall gather at His throne*

Homeless and Lonely

Try to talk, a tale, a thought
A sharing time, a moment caught

Within yourself, you yell for help
Nevertheless, who will hear but you?

Try to go to who knows where
Does it really matter how or why? who cares

A journey's end, a bend, or twist
Is that or this a reason, no matter

Summer, spring, or fall; up, or down, who cares?

Let's just do what we can, forget our plans
Improvise; be wise, or happy

There is a way, I am sure I will find it, now or later
Does it really matter?

At least I started on my way up, or was it down
Did I simply come around?

To find myself, in all I do, at least I knew
I could rely on me

So go ahead, carry on, or go ahead and scorn, be gone
For who am I that You should ponder
Wander, yonder, no one cares anyway

However, I finally feel that I know better
No one will ever know me better than I do

As A Child

Once I was a child
 I acted as a child
 I spoke as a child
 I dreamed as children dream
 I cried as children cry
 I laughed as children laugh
 I played as children play

And as I grew old
 I noticed others aged untold
 Had pride without a tear
 Had hate without any fear
 Had dreams but plowed no fields
 Had frowns that turned like wheels
 Had games no one could play
 Had rooms no one could stay
 Had time but never got there
 Had love but none to share
 Knew of God but never held Him close
 Grew old and lost in sin
 Never took time to see the Lord with us
 Or accepted His gift of grace and forgiveness

If only everyone knew of His love from deep within
 Moreover, the joy set before Him as He died for our sin

Together As His

This day I hold you close, my dear
  Together we celebrate our forever year

To renew our vows and hold you close
  In the presence of the Father, Son, and Holy Ghost

As we begin our lives and start again
  I cherish fond memories, both now and then

As we rise up together as on Eagles' Wings
  Our hearts forever rejoice and sing,

Life's' song of love He has blessed us with—as **His**

To Live Is Christ

When I was a child, I was just a child
  When I became a man, I learned to become like a child

When the wings of wisdom gently touched my
  Presence, I began to realize
  To live is Christ, to die most certainly gain

Christ has drawn me close with great love and mercy

Now it seems that with every tear I shed
  He gently wipes them with His smile

In the valley of the shadow
  I have truly heard the sound of His footsteps

His reflection upon the waters that gently flow through
  My pathways
  Have made my way clear

Raised back to life
  See the nail prints in His hands

On that special Day of Atonement
  Hanging on the cross beneath His marvelous sky

His pre-determined desire was
  While I was yet a sinner, He gave Himself for me

He oversees my way and charts my path each day
  I have risen up on the wings of God's creation

In addition, I can do all things through Christ

My heart, my hands, and my love
  Only do what He graciously allows

Weeping endures for a night
  His joy arrives fresh each morning,

As I continue my journey riding His morning winds
  I breathe His name in confidence,

Knowing He shall guide me
  For He is my all-consuming fire

My peace, my Comforter, and everlasting love
  All that I do that shines is His handiwork

All that I do that is kind is His touch of grace
  Though I write, He is the author

Though I strive, He is the finisher
  Though I live, He is the Way, the Truth, and the Life

For those who ask
  Who is this Lord of glory?

He is the precious Word of God
  Moreover, nothing will ever separate my desire
  to live is Christ

REFERENCES & CONTACT

Scripture passages cited in this book:

Exodus 23:20

Numbers 6:24-26

1 Samuel 15:22

Psalm 86:3, 86:5, 103:12, 109:12, 139:1-24

Proverbs 23:7, 28:13

Isaiah 1:18, 43:2, 59:19

Matthew 5:40-48, 6:14-15

Mark 10:25

Mark 12:28-34

Luke 5:10, 11:11-13, 15:10

John 1:1, 1:11-14, 3:16, 6:37-38, 8:7, 11:25-26, 14:1,6,27

Acts 2:21

Romans 2:6-8, 6:22, 8:28, 8:31, 10:9

1 Corinthians 15:51-58

2 Corinthians 6:14, 6:16-17

Ephesians 4:29-32, 5:22

Philippians 2:1-11, 4:11-13, 4:19

2 Timothy 3:16

Hebrews 12:2

1 Peter 2:2-3

1 John 1:9, 2:4, 3:2

Revelation 3:5

Contact information

For more information about *Tell Him With Your Heart* contact:
RAYFIKEMUSIC@GMAIL.COM

May this book encourage you to believe that you can rise up on wings as eagles, and rest in the knowledge that the love of God is above all love. If you really love the Lord, tell Him with your heart!

www.ingramcontent.com/pod-product-compliance
Lightning Source LLC
Chambersburg PA
CBHW021336090426
42742CB00008B/630